# 147 PRACTICAL TIPS FOR TEACHING SUSTAINABILITY

## *Connecting the Environment, the Economy, and Society*

by
William M. Timpson, Brian Dunbar, Gailmarie Kimmel,
Brett Bruyere, Peter Newman, and Hillary Mizia

ATWOOD PUBLISHING
Madison, Wisconsin

# DEDICATION

*In gratitude to this extraordinary planet that sustains and inspires us.
And to the teachers and learners who carry the tradition on.*

147 Tips for Teaching Sustainability
by William M. Timpson, Brian Dunbar, Gailmarie Kimmel,
Brett Bruyere, Peter Newman, and Hillary Mizia

© 2006, Atwood Publishing, Madison, WI
*www.atwoodpublishing.com*

Cover and interior design © TLC Graphics, www.TLCGraphics.com

ISBN: 978-1-891859-60-1

Library of Congress Cataloging-in-Publication Data

147 tips for teaching sustainability : connecting the environment, the
 economy, and society / by William M. Timpson ... [et al.].
     p. cm.
 Includes bibliographical references and index.
 ISBN-13: 978-1-891859-60-1 (pbk.)
 1. Environmental education.  2. Sustainable development--Study
and teaching.    I. Timpson, William M.  II. Title: One hundred
forty-seven tips for teaching sustainability.
GE70.A13 2006
338.9'27071--dc22

2006007820

# Table of Tips

Foreword by David W. Orr . . . . . . . . . . . . . . . . . . . . . . . . . . . . . . . . . . . . . . . . . . ix
Foreword by Anthony Cortese . . . . . . . . . . . . . . . . . . . . . . . . . . . . . . . . . . . . . xi
Preface. . . . . . . . . . . . . . . . . . . . . . . . . . . . . . . . . . . . . . . . . . . . . . . . . . . . . . . . . xv
Acknowledgments. . . . . . . . . . . . . . . . . . . . . . . . . . . . . . . . . . . . . . . . . . . . . . xix
List of Contributors . . . . . . . . . . . . . . . . . . . . . . . . . . . . . . . . . . . . . . . . . . . . xxi

SECTION ONE
## DEFINING SUSTAINABILITY . . . . . . . . . . . . . . . . . . . . . . . . . . . . . 1
Introduce the Notion That We Are Nature. . . . . . . . . . . . . . . . . . . . . . . . . . 1
Use the Eco-Sphere to Visualize Sustainability . . . . . . . . . . . . . . . . . . . . . 2
Create a Common Language. . . . . . . . . . . . . . . . . . . . . . . . . . . . . . . . . . . . . 3
Begin With the Fundamentals. . . . . . . . . . . . . . . . . . . . . . . . . . . . . . . . . . . 3
Help Others Listen to the Elders. . . . . . . . . . . . . . . . . . . . . . . . . . . . . . . . . 4

SECTION TWO
## HISTORICAL PERSPECTIVES . . . . . . . . . . . . . . . . . . . . . . . . . . . . 5
Make the Case for Possibility . . . . . . . . . . . . . . . . . . . . . . . . . . . . . . . . . . . 5
Add Missing Voices. . . . . . . . . . . . . . . . . . . . . . . . . . . . . . . . . . . . . . . . . . . 6
Revisit Big, Unresolved Questions. . . . . . . . . . . . . . . . . . . . . . . . . . . . . . . 6
Travel Back to the Future . . . . . . . . . . . . . . . . . . . . . . . . . . . . . . . . . . . . . . 7
Conduct the Twentieth-Century Experiment . . . . . . . . . . . . . . . . . . . . . . 7
Talk About What We Once Had . . . . . . . . . . . . . . . . . . . . . . . . . . . . . . . . . 8

SECTION THREE
## SYSTEMS, SYNERGY, AND VISIONS . . . . . . . . . . . . . . . . . . . . . 9
View the World Through a Systems Lens . . . . . . . . . . . . . . . . . . . . . . . . . . 9
Connect the Dots . . . . . . . . . . . . . . . . . . . . . . . . . . . . . . . . . . . . . . . . . . . . 10
Use Leverage Points. . . . . . . . . . . . . . . . . . . . . . . . . . . . . . . . . . . . . . . . . . 10
Recognize the Chain of Custody. . . . . . . . . . . . . . . . . . . . . . . . . . . . . . . . 11

Connect Capitalism and Sustainability . . . . . . . . . . . . . . . . . . . . . . . . . . . . . . . . . . 12
Envision Finding Your Way Out of a Disaster . . . . . . . . . . . . . . . . . . . . . . . . . . . 12
Assign a Voice for the Future . . . . . . . . . . . . . . . . . . . . . . . . . . . . . . . . . . . . . . . . 13
Seek Out Visionary Efforts . . . . . . . . . . . . . . . . . . . . . . . . . . . . . . . . . . . . . . . . . . 13
Consider the Wealth of a Nation . . . . . . . . . . . . . . . . . . . . . . . . . . . . . . . . . . . . 14

## SECTION FOUR
# ECONOMICS AND CONSUMPTION . . . . . . . . . . . . . . . . . . . . 15

Explore a Living Economy . . . . . . . . . . . . . . . . . . . . . . . . . . . . . . . . . . . . . . . . . . 15
Use an Ecological Measure of Consumption . . . . . . . . . . . . . . . . . . . . . . . . . . . 16
Change the Cost Paradigm . . . . . . . . . . . . . . . . . . . . . . . . . . . . . . . . . . . . . . . . . 16
Show How Sustainability Contributes to Staying "In the Black" . . . . . . . . . . 17
Understand Synergistic Relationships . . . . . . . . . . . . . . . . . . . . . . . . . . . . . . . . 17
Recognize the Power Of Consumers as Agents of Change. . . . . . . . . . . . . . . . 18
Promote Inclusive Prosperity. . . . . . . . . . . . . . . . . . . . . . . . . . . . . . . . . . . . . . . 18
Pick Low-Hanging Fruit First . . . . . . . . . . . . . . . . . . . . . . . . . . . . . . . . . . . . . . 19
Address Disparities . . . . . . . . . . . . . . . . . . . . . . . . . . . . . . . . . . . . . . . . . . . . . . 19
Compare Needs With Wants. . . . . . . . . . . . . . . . . . . . . . . . . . . . . . . . . . . . . . . 20
Explore Community-Based Social Marketing . . . . . . . . . . . . . . . . . . . . . . . . . 20

## SECTION FIVE
# DESIGN, NATURE, AND BUILDINGS . . . . . . . . . . . . . . . . . . . 21

See Nature as a Mentor. . . . . . . . . . . . . . . . . . . . . . . . . . . . . . . . . . . . . . . . . . . . 21
Build on Nature's Lead . . . . . . . . . . . . . . . . . . . . . . . . . . . . . . . . . . . . . . . . . . . . 22
Remember the Pen Is Mightier Than the Sword,
but the Wrench Is Mightier Still . . . . . . . . . . . . . . . . . . . . . . . . . . . . . . . . . . . . 22
Understand How Classrooms Can Teach . . . . . . . . . . . . . . . . . . . . . . . . . . . . 22
Reframe Conventional Design . . . . . . . . . . . . . . . . . . . . . . . . . . . . . . . . . . . . . 23
Create Spaces That Love You Back . . . . . . . . . . . . . . . . . . . . . . . . . . . . . . . . . . 24
"Leed" by Example . . . . . . . . . . . . . . . . . . . . . . . . . . . . . . . . . . . . . . . . . . . . . . . 24
Seek Out Buildings That Allow Students to Teach . . . . . . . . . . . . . . . . . . . . . 25
View Biology Through a New Lens. . . . . . . . . . . . . . . . . . . . . . . . . . . . . . . . . . . 26

## SECTION SIX
# ETHICS, VALUES, AND THE SACRED . . . . . . . . . . . . . . . . . . 27

Rethink Basic Rights. . . . . . . . . . . . . . . . . . . . . . . . . . . . . . . . . . . . . . . . . . . . . . 27
Nurture an Ethic for Nature . . . . . . . . . . . . . . . . . . . . . . . . . . . . . . . . . . . . . . . . 28
Explore What Informs Revered Leaders . . . . . . . . . . . . . . . . . . . . . . . . . . . . . . 28
Align Values and Actions. . . . . . . . . . . . . . . . . . . . . . . . . . . . . . . . . . . . . . . . . . 29
See Enemies as Potential Allies . . . . . . . . . . . . . . . . . . . . . . . . . . . . . . . . . . . . . 29
Plant Hope . . . . . . . . . . . . . . . . . . . . . . . . . . . . . . . . . . . . . . . . . . . . . . . . . . . . . 30
Use Precaution as Wisdom . . . . . . . . . . . . . . . . . . . . . . . . . . . . . . . . . . . . . . . . 30
Acknowledge Grief, Invite Connection . . . . . . . . . . . . . . . . . . . . . . . . . . . . . . 31

Brainstorm a "Should" List . . . . . . . . . . . . . . . . . . . . . . . . . . . . . . . . . . . . . . . . 31
Find Ways to Use Faith . . . . . . . . . . . . . . . . . . . . . . . . . . . . . . . . . . . . . . . . . . . 32
Read Sacred Texts . . . . . . . . . . . . . . . . . . . . . . . . . . . . . . . . . . . . . . . . . . . . . . . 32

SECTION SEVEN
# PERSONAL RESPONSIBILITY AND EMPOWERMENT . . . . . . . . . . . . . . . . . . . . . . . . . . . 33

Understand the Tipping Point . . . . . . . . . . . . . . . . . . . . . . . . . . . . . . . . . . . . . 33
Realize That Objects in the Mirror Are More Important Than They Appear . . . 34
Aim to Inspire . . . . . . . . . . . . . . . . . . . . . . . . . . . . . . . . . . . . . . . . . . . . . . . . . 34
Loosen Up on Expectations . . . . . . . . . . . . . . . . . . . . . . . . . . . . . . . . . . . . . . 34
Remember to Save the Humans . . . . . . . . . . . . . . . . . . . . . . . . . . . . . . . . . . . 35
Identify New Leaders . . . . . . . . . . . . . . . . . . . . . . . . . . . . . . . . . . . . . . . . . . . 35
Write the President . . . . . . . . . . . . . . . . . . . . . . . . . . . . . . . . . . . . . . . . . . . . . 36
Pause and Reflect, but Keep Moving . . . . . . . . . . . . . . . . . . . . . . . . . . . . . . . 36

SECTION EIGHT
# PLAN AHEAD . . . . . . . . . . . . . . . . . . . . . . . . . . . . . . . . . . . . . . 37

Think About Your Goals . . . . . . . . . . . . . . . . . . . . . . . . . . . . . . . . . . . . . . . . . 37
Remember There's More to Education . . . . . . . . . . . . . . . . . . . . . . . . . . . . . . 37
Take Advantage of Technology . . . . . . . . . . . . . . . . . . . . . . . . . . . . . . . . . . . . 38
Bring Your Students on Business Trips...Virtually . . . . . . . . . . . . . . . . . . . . . 38
Choose Texts Carefully . . . . . . . . . . . . . . . . . . . . . . . . . . . . . . . . . . . . . . . . . . 39

SECTION NINE
# APPROACHES AND ASSESSMENTS . . . . . . . . . . . . . . . . . . . . . . 41

Explore Multiple Approaches to Powerful Ideas . . . . . . . . . . . . . . . . . . . . . . . 41
Use Active, Student-Led Exercises . . . . . . . . . . . . . . . . . . . . . . . . . . . . . . . . . 42
Let the Poets Speak . . . . . . . . . . . . . . . . . . . . . . . . . . . . . . . . . . . . . . . . . . . . 42
Implement the Ten-Second Lab . . . . . . . . . . . . . . . . . . . . . . . . . . . . . . . . . . . 44
Use Guests and Films to Offer Diverse Perspectives . . . . . . . . . . . . . . . . . . . 44
Invent Games and Have a Little Fun . . . . . . . . . . . . . . . . . . . . . . . . . . . . . . . 45
Put on Your Guide Hat . . . . . . . . . . . . . . . . . . . . . . . . . . . . . . . . . . . . . . . . . . 45
Trust Your Gut . . . . . . . . . . . . . . . . . . . . . . . . . . . . . . . . . . . . . . . . . . . . . . . . 46
Generate New Data . . . . . . . . . . . . . . . . . . . . . . . . . . . . . . . . . . . . . . . . . . . . 46

SECTION TEN
# LEARNING THROUGH EXPERIENCE . . . . . . . . . . . . . . . . . . . 47

Experience It! . . . . . . . . . . . . . . . . . . . . . . . . . . . . . . . . . . . . . . . . . . . . . . . . . 47
Connect Learning and Service . . . . . . . . . . . . . . . . . . . . . . . . . . . . . . . . . . . . 48
Unravel the Gordian Knot . . . . . . . . . . . . . . . . . . . . . . . . . . . . . . . . . . . . . . . 48
Make It Rich and Keep It Wild . . . . . . . . . . . . . . . . . . . . . . . . . . . . . . . . . . . . 49

Take That Leap of Faith . . . . . . . . . . . . . . . . . . . . . . . . . . . . . . . . . . . . . . . 50
Question Assumptions . . . . . . . . . . . . . . . . . . . . . . . . . . . . . . . . . . . . . . . . 50
Focus the Group . . . . . . . . . . . . . . . . . . . . . . . . . . . . . . . . . . . . . . . . . . . . . 51
Focus on Investigations . . . . . . . . . . . . . . . . . . . . . . . . . . . . . . . . . . . . . . . . 51
Treat the Rest of the World Like Paradise . . . . . . . . . . . . . . . . . . . . . . . . 52
Develop Natural Schoolyards . . . . . . . . . . . . . . . . . . . . . . . . . . . . . . . . . . 53

SECTION ELEVEN
The Positive Learning Climate . . . . . . . . . . . . . . . . . . . . . . 55
Support Fair-Weather Learning . . . . . . . . . . . . . . . . . . . . . . . . . . . . . . . . . 55
Nurture a Love of Place . . . . . . . . . . . . . . . . . . . . . . . . . . . . . . . . . . . . . . . 56
Practice Acceptance . . . . . . . . . . . . . . . . . . . . . . . . . . . . . . . . . . . . . . . . . . 56
Face Problems . . . . . . . . . . . . . . . . . . . . . . . . . . . . . . . . . . . . . . . . . . . . . . . 57
Build on Peacemaking . . . . . . . . . . . . . . . . . . . . . . . . . . . . . . . . . . . . . . . . 57
Go for the "Jazz" . . . . . . . . . . . . . . . . . . . . . . . . . . . . . . . . . . . . . . . . . . . . . 58
Look Ahead With Hope . . . . . . . . . . . . . . . . . . . . . . . . . . . . . . . . . . . . . . . 58

SECTION TWELVE
AWARENESS AND CONSCIOUSNESS
EXPANSION . . . . . . . . . . . . . . . . . . . . . . . . . . . . . . . . . . . . . . . . 61
Build on Experience . . . . . . . . . . . . . . . . . . . . . . . . . . . . . . . . . . . . . . . . . 61
Take the Ecological Footprint Quiz . . . . . . . . . . . . . . . . . . . . . . . . . . . . . 62
Conduct an Ecological Footprint Audit . . . . . . . . . . . . . . . . . . . . . . . . . 62
Discuss Full-Cost Accounting . . . . . . . . . . . . . . . . . . . . . . . . . . . . . . . . . . 62
Explore What's in Everyday Products . . . . . . . . . . . . . . . . . . . . . . . . . . . . 63
Consider Scale and Energy Consumption . . . . . . . . . . . . . . . . . . . . . . . . 63
Identify Services Provided by Nature . . . . . . . . . . . . . . . . . . . . . . . . . . . . 64
Recognize That Size Matters . . . . . . . . . . . . . . . . . . . . . . . . . . . . . . . . . . . 64
Look Twice at What's Disturbing . . . . . . . . . . . . . . . . . . . . . . . . . . . . . . . 65

SECTION THIRTEEN
EFFECTIVE COMMUNICATION . . . . . . . . . . . . . . . . . . . . . . 67
Widen Participation . . . . . . . . . . . . . . . . . . . . . . . . . . . . . . . . . . . . . . . . . . 67
Emphasize Soft Skills and Hard Sciences Equally . . . . . . . . . . . . . . . . . . 68
Teach How to Negotiate . . . . . . . . . . . . . . . . . . . . . . . . . . . . . . . . . . . . . . 68
Share Like a Friend . . . . . . . . . . . . . . . . . . . . . . . . . . . . . . . . . . . . . . . . . . 68
Be Honest . . . . . . . . . . . . . . . . . . . . . . . . . . . . . . . . . . . . . . . . . . . . . . . . . . 69
Share What Has Touched You . . . . . . . . . . . . . . . . . . . . . . . . . . . . . . . . . . 69
Encourage Specificity . . . . . . . . . . . . . . . . . . . . . . . . . . . . . . . . . . . . . . . . 70
Encourage All Writing . . . . . . . . . . . . . . . . . . . . . . . . . . . . . . . . . . . . . . . . 70
Make It Worthy of Media Attention . . . . . . . . . . . . . . . . . . . . . . . . . . . . . 71

SECTION FOURTEEN
## COOPERATION AND COLLABORATION . . . . . . . . . . . . . . . 73
Turn "Bullets" Into "Bridges" . . . . . . . . . . . . . . . . . . . . . . . . . . . . . . . . 73
Play Games to Illustrate Collaboration . . . . . . . . . . . . . . . . . . . . . . . . 74
Create Community Collaborations . . . . . . . . . . . . . . . . . . . . . . . . . . . . 74
Design a Better World Together . . . . . . . . . . . . . . . . . . . . . . . . . . . . . 75
Tie Classes and Programs Together . . . . . . . . . . . . . . . . . . . . . . . . . . 76
View Conflict as Change Agent . . . . . . . . . . . . . . . . . . . . . . . . . . . . . 76

SECTION FIFTEEN
## COMMUNITY AND A SENSE OF PLACE . . . . . . . . . . . . . . . . 77
Keep It in the Neighborhood . . . . . . . . . . . . . . . . . . . . . . . . . . . . . . . 77
Get Into "We" Mode . . . . . . . . . . . . . . . . . . . . . . . . . . . . . . . . . . . . . 78
Recognize Waste . . . . . . . . . . . . . . . . . . . . . . . . . . . . . . . . . . . . . . . . 78
Trace the Roots of Lunch . . . . . . . . . . . . . . . . . . . . . . . . . . . . . . . . . . 79
Rediscover Local Agriculture . . . . . . . . . . . . . . . . . . . . . . . . . . . . . . . 79
Walk Your Watershed . . . . . . . . . . . . . . . . . . . . . . . . . . . . . . . . . . . . 79
Compost . . . . . . . . . . . . . . . . . . . . . . . . . . . . . . . . . . . . . . . . . . . . . . . 80
Think Local, Fun, High-Tech, and Free . . . . . . . . . . . . . . . . . . . . . . . 81
Enlarge Perspectives . . . . . . . . . . . . . . . . . . . . . . . . . . . . . . . . . . . . . 81

SECTION SIXTEEN
## CRITICAL AND CREATIVE THINKING . . . . . . . . . . . . . . . . . 83
Teach How to Think, Not What to Think . . . . . . . . . . . . . . . . . . . . . . 83
Get to the Root . . . . . . . . . . . . . . . . . . . . . . . . . . . . . . . . . . . . . . . . . 84
Change Periods Into Question Marks . . . . . . . . . . . . . . . . . . . . . . . . 84
Focus on Imagination . . . . . . . . . . . . . . . . . . . . . . . . . . . . . . . . . . . . 85
Go for Understanding . . . . . . . . . . . . . . . . . . . . . . . . . . . . . . . . . . . . 85
Study Controversial Issues . . . . . . . . . . . . . . . . . . . . . . . . . . . . . . . . 86
Be a Wide-Eyed Skeptic and Demand Precision . . . . . . . . . . . . . . . . 86
Investigate Campus Ecology . . . . . . . . . . . . . . . . . . . . . . . . . . . . . . . 87
Blur Lines of Distinction Between Disciplines . . . . . . . . . . . . . . . . . . 87
Use Creative Works to Spark Debate . . . . . . . . . . . . . . . . . . . . . . . . . 87
Make Debates Public and Inclusive . . . . . . . . . . . . . . . . . . . . . . . . . . 88
Progress Logically . . . . . . . . . . . . . . . . . . . . . . . . . . . . . . . . . . . . . . . 89
Teach Good Reasoning . . . . . . . . . . . . . . . . . . . . . . . . . . . . . . . . . . . 89

SECTION SEVENTEEN
## SUPPORTING CHANGE . . . . . . . . . . . . . . . . . . . . . . . . . . . . 91
Lead Reform and (R)Evolution . . . . . . . . . . . . . . . . . . . . . . . . . . . . . 91
Influence Others . . . . . . . . . . . . . . . . . . . . . . . . . . . . . . . . . . . . . . . . 92
Train Activists for Life . . . . . . . . . . . . . . . . . . . . . . . . . . . . . . . . . . . . 92

Create a Peer Culture of Behavior Change . . . . . . . . . . . . . . . . . . . . . . . . . . . . . 93
Become the Demand. . . . . . . . . . . . . . . . . . . . . . . . . . . . . . . . . . . . . . . . . . . . . 94
Envision Change. . . . . . . . . . . . . . . . . . . . . . . . . . . . . . . . . . . . . . . . . . . . . . . . 94
Use "Team Wonder Bike" as a Model . . . . . . . . . . . . . . . . . . . . . . . . . . . . . . . 95
Walk the Talk . . . . . . . . . . . . . . . . . . . . . . . . . . . . . . . . . . . . . . . . . . . . . . . . . . 95
Sweat the Small Stuff . . . . . . . . . . . . . . . . . . . . . . . . . . . . . . . . . . . . . . . . . . . 96
Be a Prayer . . . . . . . . . . . . . . . . . . . . . . . . . . . . . . . . . . . . . . . . . . . . . . . . . . . 96
Continue the Tips. . . . . . . . . . . . . . . . . . . . . . . . . . . . . . . . . . . . . . . . . . . . . . 97

Afterword by Julie Newman . . . . . . . . . . . . . . . . . . . . . . . . . . . . . . . . . . . . . . 99
Afterword by Joyce Berry . . . . . . . . . . . . . . . . . . . . . . . . . . . . . . . . . . . . . . . 103
Afterword by Hillary Mizia. . . . . . . . . . . . . . . . . . . . . . . . . . . . . . . . . . . . . . 105
Final Reflections . . . . . . . . . . . . . . . . . . . . . . . . . . . . . . . . . . . . . . . . . . . . . . 109
Appendix. . . . . . . . . . . . . . . . . . . . . . . . . . . . . . . . . . . . . . . . . . . . . . . . . . . . 113
References . . . . . . . . . . . . . . . . . . . . . . . . . . . . . . . . . . . . . . . . . . . . . . . . . . . 115
Index. . . . . . . . . . . . . . . . . . . . . . . . . . . . . . . . . . . . . . . . . . . . . . . . . . . . . . . 121

# Foreword by David W. Orr

## ALL HANDS ON DECK: TEACHING SUSTAINABILITY

What does the word *sustainability* mean to a typical high school or college student? The answer probably is "not much." For all of the learned talk about sustainability and despite the flood of ink spilled to define the term, the first generation that must confront the stark reality of the global crisis of unsustainability (what was once called "overshoot") is, I suspect, either overwhelmed by it all or just oblivious. To most, climate change, biotic impoverishment, decline of land and seas, deforestation, pollution, poverty, terrorism, and so forth seem very distant from the problems they face every day including those of drugs and violence. Their music seems to suggest a great deal of diffuse anger and confusion but little awareness of the storms ahead. Polls indicate that the goal of getting ahead economically is still much more important to most of the rising generation than that of improving the world.

Teaching about the challenges of sustainability generally can be rather like teaching health care in the emergency room of a big city hospital on a Saturday night in July—one human tragedy followed by yet another, all night long. The history of environmental policy in the United States, for

---

*David W. Orr is the Director of the Environmental Studies Program at Oberlin College.*

example, is one sorry record of thirty years of evasion on the most important issues of the time. For the young people who do study such things it must be disconcerting to learn that their future is being compromised daily by short-sightedness, greed, ignorance, and stupidity.

In my own approach to teaching environmental studies, I've found one generally dependable antidote to what is otherwise a fairly dismal pedagogical situation. The origins, not surprisingly, are in the writings of John Dewey, Alfred North Whitehead, Maria Montessori, and J. Glenn Gray. In varying ways each proposed to make learning an active engagement with the world, not merely the study of second-hand abstractions. Applied to the problems of sustainability, that approach underlies much of the green campus movement and campus ecology courses taught over the past fifteen years. In those efforts students have applied their energy and intelligence to the goal of making their college and university campuses sustainable. The scale is small enough to be understandable but large enough to be a significant model. All campuses take in energy, water, and materials and put out waste in various forms. The idea behind the green campus movement is simply to make environmental impacts transparent and thereby render them into solutions that reduce and recycle wastes, reward efficiency, eliminate carbon emissions, improve policies governing grounds management and building standards, and use institutional purchases and investments to catalyze sustainable local economies. But this is a means to the larger end of equipping young people with the analytical skills and wherewithal to become change agents beyond the years of formal education.

From the beginning of the campus ecology movement in 1987 to the present, hundreds of institutions have begun the process of transformation. Beyond some tipping point they become what Peter Senge calls "learning organizations" that calibrate their mission and operations with the larger biophysical realities of the Earth. Many of the most exciting experiments in sustainability are being led by students and recent graduates still in their twenties who are helping to fill a vacuum of leadership in the society. They are helping to lead the effort to reduce carbon emissions, promote renewable energy, build high performance buildings, and eliminate waste. Instead of the typical career path that defers leadership to the later stages of life, they've recognized the emergency of the twenty-first century for what it is. In naval terms it is time to get all hands on deck to join the fight for a habitable planet. And when the fight is joined, real learning begins.

# Foreword by Anthony Cortese

## HIGHER EDUCATION AND SUSTAINABILITY

Higher education has been granted a unique role by society. It has been grant-ed tax-free status, the ability to receive public and private funds, and academ-ic freedom in exchange for educating students and producing the knowledge that will result in a thriving and civil society. Higher education is facing its greatest challenge in living up to its responsibility because humanity is at a crossroads. For the first time in human history, humans are pervasive and dominant forces in the health and well-being of the earth and its inhabitants. We are the first generation capable of determining the habitability of the plan-et for humans and other species. No part of the earth is unaffected by humans, and the scale of our impact is huge and growing exponentially. (The Innuits in Alaska have the highest level of PCBs and DDT in their bodies in the world, despite being one thousand miles from any industrial activity.)

Despite all the work we have done on environmental protection, all living sys-tems are in long-term decline and are declining at an increasing rate accord-ing to all international scientific, health, and policy organizations. This is happening with 20% of the world's population consuming 80% of the world's resources. How will we cope in a world that *will* have nine billion people and that plans to increase GWP by 500% by 2050? This is an awesome ethical

*Anthony Cortese is President of Second Nature.*

responsibility for us, especially in higher education, and teachers at every level can play an important role in helping us find that sustainable path.

As Einstein said, "We can't solve today's problems at the same level of thinking at which they were created." We need an unprecedented shift in the way we think and act. We currently view health, social, economic, political, security, population, environmental, and other major societal issues as separate, competing, and hierarchical when they are really systemic and interdependent. For example, we do not have environmental problems, per se. We have negative environmental consequences of the way we have designed our social, economic, and political systems. *We have a de facto systems design failure.* The twenty-first-century challenges must be addressed in a systemic, integrated, and holistic fashion. *Sustainability requires that we focus simultaneously on implementing systemic changes that improve health for current and future humans; building strong, secure, and thriving communities; and providing economic opportunity for all by restoring and preserving the integrity of the life support system.*

Higher education plays a critical but often overlooked role in making this vision a reality. It prepares most of the professionals who develop, lead, manage, teach, work in, and influence society's institutions, including the most basic foundation of K-12 education. Besides training future teachers, higher education strongly influences the learning framework of K-12 education, which is largely geared toward subsequent higher education. Starting in seventh grade, students start learning in silos in order to get into college. For the first time in U.S. history, seventy percent of children in the K-12 system intend to go to college. Moreover, given the need for a much more highly skilled workforce for the twenty-first century, lifelong education becomes another critical role for higher education.

However, the current educational system is reinforcing the current unhealthy, inequitable, and unsustainable path that society is pursuing. The people who are leading most of society's institutions down this path are graduates of the best colleges, universities, and professional schools in the world. *As David Orr says, the crisis humanity is facing is a "crisis of mind, perception and heart.* It is not a problem IN education; it is a problem OF education...." This is not intentional—it is a function of a worldview that is no longer suitable for creating a world that works for everyone. Higher education, following and enabling this worldview, is generally organized into highly specialized areas of knowledge and traditional disciplines. Designing a sustainable human future requires a paradigm shift toward a systemic perspective emphasizing interdisciplinary understanding, collaboration, and cooperation that must be led by higher education.

What if higher education were to take a leadership role, as it did in the space race and the war on cancer, in preparing students and providing the information and knowledge to achieve a just and sustainable society? The education of all professionals would reflect a new approach to learning and practice. A college or university would operate as a fully integrated community that models social and biological sustainability itself and in its interdependence with the local, regional, and global community. In many cases, we think of teaching, research, operations, and relations with local communities as separate activities; they are not.

All parts of the university are critical in helping to create transformative change in the individual and collective mindset. Everything that happens at a university and every impact, positive and negative, of university activities shapes the knowledge, skills, and values of the students. Future education must connect head, heart, and hand. The educational experience of graduates must reflect an intimate connection among *curriculum* and (1) research; (2) understanding and reducing any negative ecological and social footprint of the institution; and (3) working to improve local and regional communities so that they are healthier, more socially vibrant and stable, economically secure, and environmentally sustainable.

Just imagine if, in the twenty-first century, the educational experience of all students is aligned with the principles of sustainability. To achieve this, the following elements will need to be in place:

- The *content of learning* will reflect interdisciplinary systems thinking, dynamics, and analysis for all majors, disciplines, and professional degrees—education would have the same *lateral rigor* across as the *vertical rigor* within the disciplines.

- The *context of learning* will change to make human/environment interdependence, values, and ethics a seamless and central part of teaching all disciplines, rather than isolated as a special course or module in programs for specialists. All students will understand that we are an integral part of nature. They will understand the ecological services that are critical for human existence, how to all the health, social, economic, and environmental impacts visible and as positive as possible.

- The *process of education* will emphasize active, experiential, inquiry-based learning and real-world problem solving on the campus and in the larger community.

- Higher education will *practice sustainability*. Campuses will "practice what they preach" and make sustainability an integral part of *operations, planning, facility design, purchasing, and investments*, and tie these efforts to the formal curriculum. The university is a microcosm of the larger community. Therefore, the manner in which it carries out its daily activities is an important demonstration of ways to achieve environmentally responsible living and to reinforce desired values and behaviors in the whole community. *These activities provide unparalleled opportunities for teaching, research, and learning.*

- Higher education will form *partnerships with local and regional communities* to help make them healthy, socially vibrant, economically secure, and environmentally sustainable as an integral part of higher education's mission and the student experience. Higher education institutions are anchor institutions for economic development in most of their communities, especially now that the private sector moves facilities, capital, and jobs frequently as mergers, acquisitions, and globalization become the norm for corporations. The four thousand higher education institutions in the United States are, themselves, large economic engines with annual operational budgets totaling three hundred billion dollars in 2003. This is greater than the GDP of all but twenty-five countries in the world.

The issue is not the ability of higher education to take on this challenge. It is the will and the timeframe of doing so. *If higher education does not lead the sustainability effort in society, who will?*

Fortunately, there are hundreds of examples of changes in higher education activities that shape the total student experience. These examples are available through the new Association for Advancement of Sustainability in Higher Education (www.aashe.org); Second Nature publications; Second Nature's web site; and a number of other organizations, such as NWF Campus Ecology Program (www.nwf.org/campusecology); and University Leaders for a Sustainable Future (www.ulsf.org).

The most successful changes are those in which the formal curriculum is an integral part of the other functions of higher education. Most are driven by faculty and student pressure but, fortunately, an increasing number are driven by high-level academic administrators and operations executives. The biggest remaining challenge is the reorientation of the curriculum. Higher education is perilously slow in this arena. *147 Tips for Teaching Sustainability* is a critically important guide for faculty and others that will greatly enhance the ability of higher education as well as other organizations to make sustainability the goal of learning and practice.

# *Preface*

At its core, this book is about empowerment, facing reality, and learning to think and act with greater reverence for Earth, its limits, and its intelligence, and then teaching others to do the same. Sustainability is one of those big, complex concepts that defy easy definition or simple responses, yet demand attention for our collective well-being. It affects all of us, regardless of our background, age, political affiliation, geography, or other characteristics. It requires cooperation and collaboration from ecologists, sociologists, economists, community leaders, business leaders, and many, many others who have not historically worked together.

If you address these concepts, then teaching about sustainability can be truly transformative and can challenge people of all ages and backgrounds to think and act in very new ways. In what follows, we offer you a range of concise, practical tips for the following activities:

- Rethinking some of our most basic assumptions
- Considering creative solutions
- Communicating honestly and navigating emotions
- Balancing challenges with a realistic optimism

In his landmark *Earth in Mind*, David Orr sounds the alarm about expanding human populations and our appetite for resources juxtaposed with our short-sightedness about Earth's limits. In *Natural Capitalism*, Paul Hawken, Amory Lovins, and Hunter Lovins describe the growing threat to our collective health from mining Earth's resources without any economic or social calculation for the effect of resulting toxic wastes. This physical damage to the environment is also rippling back on us in ever larger social and economic tsunamis. If these authors are right—and the latest edition of State of the

World by the Worldwatch Institute confirms these trends—then our own work on teaching sustainability in all areas of life is especially crucial and germane. As Orr states, "It is not education, but education of a certain kind, that will save us" (Orr 1994, 8).

*147 Tips for Teaching Sustainability* presents ideas and strategies for addressing tough, compelling issues in practical and effective ways. Our team of contributors included scholars; teachers and students; and local business people; as well as representatives from non-profit organizations working locally, nationally, and globally. This book was very much a community effort, just as sustainability can, and must, be a community effort that starts with the local community and has global effects.

## THE TRIPLE BOTTOM LINE

This community effort became especially important as we pushed past our individual disciplinary "silos" and focused on sustainability as a reflection of environmental, economic, and societal factors. As every ecologist will insist, a more holistic, interconnected perspective makes sense in both practical and theoretical terms. Complex topics resist simplistic, reductionistic analyses and, instead, require sophisticated, interdisciplinary thinking and creativity. And so it is with the study of sustainability.

## WHY "TIPS" AND WHY 147?

Anyone who teaches appreciates the value of an idea that is practical and concrete—something that can be tried, adapted, and assessed. We understand that many teachers become impatient with theories that lack applicability. However, we also recognize the limitations of any cookbook that only offers recipes and no explanations that would permit adaptation or further experimentation. The best analogy we have is when teachers emphasize memorization for objective tests without any real commitment to promoting a deeper understanding. Likewise, everyone has been frustrated by students, coworkers, or others who seem unable to adapt their learning for new challenges. The sources we include in many of our tips give you rich resources to tap as you move forward. As Jared Diamond concludes in *Collapse*, the test of every culture is whether it will adapt to whatever threats emerge, or wither and disappear.

As for the number 147? Other books on teaching offer some round number of tips. Very simply, the first in this series came to 147, so our publisher took it on as a signature marker.

## CONCEPTS AND STRATEGIES

Underlying our own "tips for teaching sustainability" are a number of core concepts that define sustainability:

- Underlying systems thinking
- Interconnections between the natural world and human societies
- Ethics, values, and the sacred
- Learning from nature
- Best use of technology
- Role of personal responsibility and empowerment
- Collective need for new visions

For these concepts, we are indebted to the pioneering work of Second Nature in articulating a direction for higher education to address sustainability. Instead of bringing these concepts into every tip, however, we offer concise, accessible explanations along with a recommended activity so that you can see an idea in practice and learn through experience. Many colleagues contributed to this process and are noted in the text.

We also recommend strategies for teaching important aspects of sustainability:

- How cooperative and collaborative learning become important for emphasizing principles of interconnectedness
- How discovery learning can equip people to address complex and challenging problems
- How the use of experiential learning can get students out into the natural world
- How learning can be deepened by putting lessons into practice

## RESPONSIBILITY AND COURAGE

As a final thought, we turn to the Preamble to the Earth Charter that first appeared at the Earth Summit in Rio de Janeiro in 1992: "We stand at a critical moment in Earth's history, a time when humanity must choose its future.... We must join together to bring forth a sustainable global society founded on respect for nature, universal human rights, economic justice, and a culture of peace" (Earth Charter Initiative 2000). We hope that our own book will bring something new and useful to this challenge we all share.

# Acknowledgments

## SCHOOL OF EDUCATION, COLORADO STATE UNIVERSITY

- Cliff Harbour (Community College Leadership)
- *Graduate students:* Karyn Madison and Jill Charbonneau (Design and Merchandising); Elizabeth Sink (Speech Communication); Kevin Murray (high school science teacher, Greeley, CO); Catherine Richardson and Jen Fullerton (Organizational Development, Performance and Change); Chris Odell (Exercise and Sport Science, Metropolitan State College); Annie Showalter (Foreign Languages); Andrew Medina (elementary school teacher, Jefferson County, CO); Kay Rios (Journalism); Michelle Hickey-Gramke (Educational Leadership); Tim Pearson (elementary school teacher, Fort Collins, CO)

## WARNER COLLEGE OF NATURAL RESOURCES, COLORADO STATE UNIVERSITY

- Tony Cheng (Forest, Rangeland and Watershed Stewardship)
- Del Benson (Fishery and Wildlife Biology)
- *Students:* Tara Peterson, Bristole McFee, Kit Benshoof, Sarah Schweizer, Aimee Chlebnik, Roderic Rosario, Cody Bride, Drew Erickson, Cody Kremer

## OTHER UNITS AT COLORADO STATE UNIVERSITY

- Rod Adams (Philosophy)
- David Gunderson (Construction Management)
- Ray Aberle (Challenge Ropes Course)
- Josie Plaut (Institute for the Built Environment)
- Jennifer Walton (Environmental Communications)

## OTHER UNIVERSITIES

- C. Bruce Martin (Sport and Exercise Science, University of Northern Colorado)
- Jane Ahrens (Architecture, University of Texas at Arlington)

- Katy Janda (Environmental Sciences, Oberlin College)
- William Doe (Environmental Studies, Western Illinois University)
- Heather McIlvaine-Newsad (Anthropology, Western Illinois University)
- Robert Ernst (President, Northcentral Technical College, Wisconsin)
- Chris Romero (Biology, Front Range Community College)
- Mike Montoya (Construction Management, California Polytechnical Institute)

## POUDRE SCHOOL DISTRICT, FORT COLLINS, COLORADO
- Marlon Poole (Environmental Studies, Poudre High School)
- Diane Odbert (Fifth grade teacher, Bacon Elementary School)
- Mike Spearnak (Chief Architect)

## NONPROFIT ORGANIZATIONS
- David Bartecchi (Program Director, Village Earth)
- Richard Fox (Co-Director, Trees, Water & People)
- Bryan Birch (Education Director, Rocky Mountain Sustainable Living Fair)
- Ben Lawhon (Education Director, Leave No Trace Center for Outdoor Ethics)

## NEW BELGIUM BREWING COMPANY, FORT COLLINS, COLORADO
- Alie Sweany (Environmental Health and Safety)
- David Dimatteo (The Liquid Center Leader)
- Alli Aichinger (The Liquid Center and Quality Assurance)
- Meredith Giske (Marketing Manager)
- Bryan Simpson (Media Relations)

## NATIONAL PARK SERVICE
- Richard Gilliland and Jeff Maugans (Rocky Mountain National Park)

## OTHER CONTRIBUTORS
- John Mlade (Sustainability Coordinator, Perkins and Will Architects, Atlanta, GA)
- David Schaller (Coordinator for Sustainable Development, Environmental Protection Agency, Region 8)
- Alison Mason (Principal, SunJuice)

## EDITORIAL AND PUBLISHING ASSISTANCE
- Kellee Timpson (Glacier, WA)
- Karen Marcus (Final Draft Communications, Fort Collins, CO)

# List of Contributors

*William M. Timpson, Ph.D.*, is a professor in the School of Education at Colorado State University (CSU). After receiving his Bachelor's degree in American History from Harvard University, Bill went on to teach junior and senior high school in the inner city of Cleveland, Ohio before completing a doctoral degree in educational psychology at the University of Wisconsin, Madison. Along with numerous articles, chapters, and grants, he has written or coauthored ten other books including *Stepping Up: College Learning and Community for a Sustainable Future* (2001) and *147 Practical Tips for Teaching Diversity* (2005). You can e-mail Bill at *wtimpson@lamar.colostate.edu*.

*Brian Dunbar, LEED-AP*, is director of the CSU Institute for the Built Environment (IBE), and associate professor in the Department of Construction Management. Brian is the primary instructor for the IBE's Green Building Certificate program, which teaches students skills and knowledge in sustainable building practices. His teaching and design projects have received numerous local, regional, and national awards. You can e-mail Brian at *dunbar@ cahs.colostate.edu*.

*Gailmarie Kimmel, M.Ed., M.A.*, brings thirty years of experience in community and university education. After participating in the Peace Corps, she staffed Peace and Conflict Studies at University of California at Berkeley and two Oakland churches, cofounded a multidisciplinary think tank, and directed an environmental camp. Currently, she works with the CSU Forest Service, linking sustainable land management with green building and bioenergy, and coordinates the Green Building Certificate Program for CSU's IBE. She serves on the Board of Directors for the Rocky Mountain Sustainable Living Association and is launching its local living economy project. You can e-mail Gailmarie at *gmkimmel@colostate.edu.*

*Brett Bruyere, Ph.D.,* is director of the CSU Environmental Learning Center (ELC) and assistant professor in the Department of Natural Resource Recreation and Tourism. The ELC provides programs to thousands of students, families, and educators annually about environmental conservation. You can e-mail Brett at *bruyere@lamar.colostate.edu.*

*Peter Newman, Ph.D.,* is an assistant professor of protected areas management at the Warner College of Natural Resources at CSU. His research focuses on the human dimensions of natural resources management and visitor carrying capacity in the context of protected areas management. He also has work experience as a National Park Service Ranger in the Division of Resources Management in Yosemite National Park and as a naturalist/instructor for the Yosemite Institute. You can e-mail Peter at *pnewman@warnercnr.colostate.edu.*

*Hillary Mizia* is the Sustainability Coordinator for New Belgium Brewing Company, where her love and talent for educating about the environment is manifested on a daily basis. She holds a Bachelor of Arts in Experiential Education from Prescott College, and a Master of Arts in Environment and Community from Antioch University, Seattle. She currently serves on the Board of Directors for the Rocky Mountain Sustainable Living Association and for the Big Thompson Watershed Forum. She currently lives at, plays in, and telecommutes from her home in Golden, CO with her husband, son, and two dogs. You can e-mail Hillary at *hmizia@newbelgium.com.*

# *Defining Sustainability*

The forces that determine sustainability are so diverse that a clear and inclusive definition is especially important for teaching and learning.

## 1. Introduce the Notion That We Are Nature

Point out that our everyday actions contribute to creating a sustainable world just as much as big sustainability projects. Encourage people to see every aspect of their surroundings as the "environment."

Assistant professor Peter Newman notes, "When we discuss the environment we should always acknowledge that humans are one member of a complex, interconnected system." Brett Bruyere, Director of Colorado State University's Environmental Learning Center, adds, "Going on a field trip to some natural area may mean that students only associate 'environment' with something to be visited outside of town. It is essential to realize that the 'environment' is all around us. It's our cities and towns. It's the storm water running to our streams and rivers, the trees that mitigate air pollution." Ask students to list three things they could do today to contribute to the health of their immediate environment.

## 2. Use the Eco-Sphere to Visualize Sustainability

Use the Eco-Sphere to introduce the concept of sustainability. Refer to the model in discussions and assignments as a tool to ensure sustainability is holistically considered.

Brian Dunbar directs the Institute for the Built Environment at Colorado State University and created a graphic model, the Eco-Sphere, that reveals the many facets and subtopics embedded within sustainability. The center of the Eco-Sphere is a set of core dynamics, often referred to as the "triple bottom line" or the "three Es," Economy, Equity (society), and Ecology (environment). In this model, the 3-E core is overlaid on the built environment and is further imbedded with five outer dimensions of Nature, Energy, Health,

Culture, and Economics. Each of these five dimensions is, then, expanded in concentric rings of text, illustrating major and minor aspects of that dimension. This model has proven useful as an instructional tool for illustrating and developing a functional understanding of sustainability. Reframe a problem or issue important to your students or group as an opportunity, a challenge, and a potential source of synergistic collaboration across differences. Using the Eco-Sphere, have everyone assess the skills they need to accomplish this reframing, the skills they currently have, and what they will need to develop.

# 3. Create a Common Language

Analyze the language and concepts you use with others, taking care not to ignore those with which you disagree. Identify where definitions are needed to remove obstacles to understanding. The word "sustainability" means different things to different people. You will navigate the seas of sustainability more easily if you define the word for yourself and are open to sharing your definition with others.

New Belgium Brewing Company in Fort Collins, CO worked with a team of consultants to help employees understand the word "sustainability" for themselves as well as for the brewery. The following definition is a result of that process: "Sustainability is achieving a balanced union of ecological harmony, social respect and economic vitality. For New Belgium, it is the energy source that turns our company purpose and core values and beliefs from high-minded notions into daily visionary practices." Once the company had this common definition, it was able to move forward with a common understanding. If we want to create change, we must strive to understand each other and develop a common language. Ask students to think of three words having to do with sustainability that could be easily misunderstood. Discuss how to clarify them when talking with others.

# 4. Begin With the Fundamentals

Teach about basic environmental, economic, and social concepts that provide a foundation for understanding the larger picture of sustainability so you can move on to discuss more complex topics.

In *Earth in Mind*, David Orr (1994) identifies ten concepts that he argues all college graduates should understand: (1) the laws of thermodynamics, (2) basic principles of ecology, (3) carrying capacity, (4) energetics, (5) least-cost and end-use analysis, (6) limits of technology, (7) appropriate scale, (8) sustainable agriculture and forestry, (9) steady-state economics, and (10) environmental ethics. Assign students to research one of these concepts or argue for others and make brief presentations to their peers. You can also ask students or others to apply these concepts to their own lives.

# 5. Help Others Listen to the Elders

Dig into the literature and journals of people "on the margins" and from indigenous cultures to discover the wisdom of their respected elders. Imagine dialogues with those people about the future of human society.

Oren Lyons, Faithkeeper of the Turtle Clan, Onondaga Council of Chiefs of the Hau de no sau nee, gave an address to World Bank on October 3, 1995, entitled, "Ethics and Spiritual Values and the Promotion of Environmentally Sustainable Development." He said, "The democratic laws of most indigenous peoples arise from their understanding of the natural law and the regenerative powers that sustain life. Therefore, 'sustainable' in our terms means working with these laws that could be termed spiritual. We were instructed to make all of our laws in concert with these principles thus insuring life in endless cycles. To challenge these cycles and the interdependent processes of life that sustain us will insure our defeat and demise on this Earth" (Lyons 1996). What other ideas from elders can students find that are applicable to their current studies?

# Historical Perspectives

In the museum at the Auschwitz death camps in Poland, visitors are confronted by George Santayana's stark reminder: "Those who do not study history are condemned to repeat its failures." We and those we teach must apply the same principle to sustainability.

## 6. Make the Case for Possibility

Find evidence that supports the need for transformation. Information overload and the constant drumbeat of negative news can overwhelm even the most informed citizen. Help students and others in the community remember there is hope.

Lester Brown is president of the Earth Policy Institute and author of *Plan B: Rescuing a Planet Under Stress and a Civilization in Trouble*. In response to all those who seem paralyzed by the changes needed to support a truly sustainable culture, he reminds us of the transformation of U.S. industry after the Japanese attacks on Pearl Harbor and the American entry into World War II: "In retrospect, the speed of the conversion from a peacetime to a wartime economy was stunning.... The harnessing of U.S. industrial power tipped the scales decisively toward the Allied Forces, reversing the tide of war....The mobilization of resources within a matter of months demonstrates that an economy and, indeed, the world can restructure its economy quickly if it is convinced of the need to do so…" (Brown 2003, 205–206). Brainstorm with your students ways in which citizens can be convinced of the need for a more sustainable way of life. Remember that to convince someone of something, it is often necessary to answer the question they will inevitably ask: "What's in it for me?"

# 7. Add Missing Voices

Read passages from classics like *Sand County Almanac, Silent Spring, Nature, My Summer in the Sierras*, and others for ideas that may be missing from today's conversations. Also identify those individuals, those metaphorical "canaries," who have been warning us about unsustainability in the "mines" of our lives and offering new solutions. Encourage students to read these works as well, and infuse your talks with new insights and discoveries.

Teaching and learning are dynamic activities that can be energized by making traditional content more relevant to today's concerns about sustainability. Be sure to look through the classics as well as unpublished or neglected sources when you look for new ideas. Know that Aldo Leopold (a forester), Rachel Carson (a biologist), Ralph Waldo Emerson (a minister), John Muir (a naturalist), and many others who advocated for conservation early on were in the minority in their thinking. Discuss how people with such different backgrounds could draw such similar conclusions. Analyze why their message eventually resonated with so many people, and consider who will emerge as a conservation leader from today's legions of thinkers, scholars, and writers.

# 8. Revisit Big, Unresolved Questions

Challenge students to link past and lost opportunities to today's need for more sustainable solutions.

In *Collapse*, his compelling and sobering review of societies that faced challenges and adapted or perished, Jared Diamond asks us to study the record of human response and reflect on those environmental issues that we face today. How will history judge our actions or inactions? Diamond writes, "Greenland provides us with our closest approximation to a controlled experiment in collapse: two societies (Norse and Inuit) sharing the same island, but with very different cultures, such that one of those societies survived while the other was dying. Thus, Greenland's history conveys the message that, even in a harsh environment, collapse isn't inevitable but depends on a society's choices" (Diamond 2005, 21). According to Diamond, the Norse were so secure in their superiority over the Inuit that they refused to adopt the Inuit's time-tested, but presumably more primitive, practices for survival. Ask students to explore the question of what is happening today that history may some day judge foolish or dangerous?

# 9. Travel Back to the Future

When facing complex and difficult challenges, look to history for moments when different beliefs and values aligned to fashion more sustainable solutions. Examine the patterns in your own discipline when breakthrough thinking occurred.

The Great Depression challenged some of the most entrenched values and belief structures in the United States and led to huge shifts in policy and practices. Connecting the changes then with what is happening today reveals lessons that Alexander Keyssar finds sobering. He writes, "The New Deal was a turning point not just because of the specific, permanent programs that the federal government adopted, but also because it expressed a new, dominant consensus about social justice and the role of government. The poverty of millions of Americans was viewed as a collective responsibility rather than an assembly of individual misfortunes or failures; and it became the responsibility of government to actively combat that poverty…. Perhaps the most disturbing fact that Hurricane Katrina has placed before our eyes is our society's loss of faith in its ability to truly help the people…" (Keyssar 2005, B7–B8). What events other than the Great Depression and Hurricane Katrina have been eye openers for a large part of the population? What positive results have come out of these events?

# 10. Conduct the Twentieth-Century Experiment

Identify what has changed in your field over the past one hundred years. Consider the gains and losses. Has the growth and change been sustainable?

An environmental professional writes, "This last hundred years has been a time of unprecedented growth and change. Over this short time period, we have seen the emergence of cars and planes as well as flights to the moon and beyond. We now live in a time of rapidly evolving technologies: computers, the internet, e-mail, cell phones, television, radio, and more. We are constantly stretched to handle all this information in an increasingly fast world. Yet, how fast can we adapt? Could our overstressed processing systems somehow figure into the epidemic of so-called chronic fatigue or ADD (Attention Deficit Disorder)? I read that Prince Charles recently said, 'If you make everything over-efficient, you suck out every last drop of what up to now has been known as culture.' The desire of many people to 'return to simpler times' may well be the species crying out as more parts of the cultural 'operating system' begin to overheat and struggle for balance." Discuss what has changed in the areas of environmentalism, economics, and society.

# 11. Talk About What We Once Had

Identify those areas of your own discipline that once represented more sustainable practices.

Bryan Birch, Educational Coordinator for the Rocky Mountain Sustainable Living Association, comments, "If our colleges and universities could award honorary degrees for sustainability, then many would go to indigenous farmers from the past. Indonesian rice farmers, for example, selected out hundreds of varieties of rice based on their resistance to various diseases, drought, or monsoon rains as well as for their benefits to lactating women." What positive forces for sustainability are already in place around the world? In your community?

# Systems, Synergy, and Visions

Sustainability represents an interconnectedness of factors and forces—environmental, economic, and societal—that require new and more sophisticated analyses, teachings, and interventions. Using "systems thinking" provides a useful structure. In order to truly live in balance with the carrying capacity of Earth, we will also need deep changes in our values, thinking, and behavior. Those changes will be, in part, a product of clarifying what that sustainable future can and should be.

## 12. View the World Through a Systems Lens

Challenge narrow, disciplinary, short-term approaches with systems thinking.

David Schaller, Sustainable Development Coordinator for Region 8 of the Environmental Protection Agency, writes, "Everything in nature is connected. Nature is constantly making itself anew and taking itself apart again for the benefit of the larger system. There is never any waste or unemployment in nature. In nature, change is constant but the time scales are often long and the feedback loops difficult to observe. We need to slow down and observe so that we can see the causes and effects of the change that is going on around and under us, and thus understand better the richness of the systems framework. Adapt exercises to stretch and build learning and systems thinking capabilities by using *The Systems Thinking Playbook* (see www.sustainer.org)."

# 13. Connect the Dots

Identify the interplay of factors that underlies problems and possible solutions. Concerns about environmental justice force us to see the related factors that prevent appropriate solutions.

The "cancer alley" of Louisiana's petrochemical industries has left many in the poorest African American communities there facing the deadliest environmental and health hazards with few apparent economic possibilities for sustainable solutions. Robert Bullard is an associate professor at Clark Atlanta University's Environmental Justice Resource Center. In the immediate aftermath of Hurricane Katrina, he noted that problems of social class, ethnicity, and environmental threats were already evident in the 1970s when his study unearthed a troubling fact: "Every one of the city-owned landfills was located in a predominantly black neighborhood even though blacks made up a quarter of the population.... The hurricane highlighted some glaring inequities that most people would not see just by visiting the French Quarter. The fact is, New Orleans is 67 percent black, and almost half the children live below the poverty level. The issues of race and poverty are out of the closet, and we can no longer deny that we've done a lousy job addressing the environmental, as well as economic and social issues, in this country.... Katrina supports what environmental-justice activists have been saying for more than three decades: When you connect the dots and look at the facts, it's irrefutable that all communities are not created equal. If a community happens to be poor, or a community of color, or located on the wrong side of the tracks, it gets unequal protection" (Bullard 2005, 28–29). In what other scenarios can social blocks to sustainability be seen?

# 14. Use Leverage Points

We live in a system. We work in a system. Our economy, government, and environment are all systems. This realization can be overwhelming and confusing; it can make anyone feel inadequate and unable to influence change. Have students and others identify leverage points—places where change can be effected—in familiar systems such as their schools, colleges, universities, businesses, homes, or other entities.

In an essay entitled "Places to Intervene in a System" that appeared in the 1997 Winter edition of the *Whole Earth Review*, the late Donella Meadows identified important leverage points in systems:

- Numbers (subsidies, taxes, standards)
- Material stocks and flows
- Regulating negative feedback loops
- Driving positive feedback loops
- Information flows
- Rules of the system (incentives, punishment, constraints)
- Power of self-organization
- Goals of the system
- Mindset or paradigm out of which the goals, rules, and feedback structure arise

By exploring these leverage points, we are better able to understand how our actions (or inactions) affect systems. For example, how would a change in the mission of a local company affect the way it interacts with the local and global environment, economy, and society?

# 15. Recognize the Chain of Custody

Identify steps in the life cycle of a natural product or in the process flow of a business or home.

Tony Cheng teaches forest policy and notes, "I use a simple tool called 'concept mapping.' Concept maps, also called mind maps, situation maps, or cognitive maps, are a non-linear graphic way to depict the interrelationships, feedback loops, and linkages of a system. It is literally a series of boxes, bubbles, and interconnecting lines. Students develop chain of custody concept maps in small groups in order to learn from one another and build a common appreciation for the complex world in which they live. An easy example is making a cup of coffee. Starting from the bean on the tree, the inputs for growing the tree as well as the waste products from coffee plantations, students draw on their knowledge and imagination to track how the bean goes from the tree to a cup of coffee. They must identify the various energy, labor, chemical, and other inputs as well all the waste outputs for each link in the coffee bean's chain of custody. Once my students understand all this about the cup of coffee, they can move to more involved processes, such as lumber for their housing or the textiles that make up their wardrobes. They gain some appreciation for the complexity in these systems as well as some real skill for analysis."

# 16. Connect Capitalism and Sustainability

Examine how capitalist and democratic ideals and sustainable practices interact with each other. Richard Fox, with the non-profit organization, Trees, Water, & People, reminds us: "Democracy is not something we made *once*. It is an ongoing evolving experiment in working collectively; *we* are the ones on the cutting edge of that powerful force."

As an example, Fox points to the fundamental question of water and asks: "Is clean and sufficient water a human right that government should provide or a commodity that can be sold to the highest bidder? In the U.S., we face our own version of water privatization but for us it comes in the form of bottled water. If you look at any convenience store, you will see that we have somehow accepted the marketed premise that we should pay more for a gallon of water than we do for gasoline. Think about that! Worse yet, as people turn to bottled water as the solution for a perceived failure of our public water systems, we have less money to improve those very public water systems under question. Instead, we are now faced with a huge new form of trash (i.e., mountains of plastic bottles). The truth is that we don't adequately fund our water systems. However, the real irony is that many tests are showing that some of the bottled water is no better than the water we get from the tap or, in some cases, it is tap water but sold with a fancy label." For insight into the international debate, read *Blue Gold: The Fight to Stop Corporate Theft of the World's Water* by Maude Barlow and Tony Clarke, or view the film "Thirst" (see www.pbs.org/pov/pov2004/thirst). In what other ways does the current economic system thwart sustainability?

# 17. Envision Finding Your Way Out of a Disaster

Many communities have the opportunity to remake themselves in a different mold following the damage caused by natural disasters. What would happen if your own community was impacted? Work with others to imagine how it could be redesigned to be more in harmony with the environment, more supportive of healthy communities, and more equitable in its distribution of resources.

One educator is fond of repeating, "The stone age didn't end because of the lack of rocks! In advocating for new ways to think and act, it's easy to hang on to what you fear might be lost in the transition. However, the benefits of a sustainable economy and healthy environment will only happen when we move past the 'unsustainable stones' of waste, exploitation, and unfairness." Ask yourself what "stones" need to be removed for your own area or community to repair damages from the past and move toward sustainability.

# 18. Assign a Voice for the Future

In a discussion or debate, assign one individual to be the "advocate" or "watchdog" for future generations, offering perspectives and insights that might otherwise be missed.

Accountability is an essential component of any discussion about sustainability. As a business, program, or organization, it is tempting to grow too fast or too big. That growth can have adverse economic, social, and ecological impacts. Putting someone in the role of "defender of future generations" gives the future a voice for asking about the impact of various decisions on our economy, community, and natural environment years from now. When someone is given the license to look ahead and serve as a spokesperson for the planet, the insights that arise are often remarkable. For example, in a discussion about a proposed commercial development, designate someone to "speak for the watershed" or be a "spokesperson for the migratory birds."

# 19. Seek Out Visionary Efforts

Take a breather from the details and the numbers, the data and the critiques. Go web surfing to research inspiring organizations and dig into their founding principles and current activities to assist your own understanding about sustainability. Here are three to get you started:

*For all, The Earth Charter:* A "declaration of fundamental principles for building a just, sustainable, and peaceful global society in the 21st century. It seeks to inspire in all peoples a new sense of global interdependence and shared responsibility for the well being of the human family and the larger living world. It is an expression of hope and a call to help create a global partnership at a critical juncture in history" (www.earthcharter.org).

*For business and government, The Natural Step:* A science and systems-based approach to organizational planning for sustainability that provides a practical set of design criteria that can be used to direct social, environmental, and economic actions (www.naturalstep.org).

*For higher education, The Talloires Declaration:* A ten-point action plan for incorporating sustainability and environmental literacy in teaching, research, operations, and outreach at colleges and universities. It has been signed by over three hundred university presidents and chancellors in over forty countries (www.ulsf.org).

# 20. Consider the Wealth of a Nation

Offer a broader definition of genuine wealth focusing on five key asset areas: human, natural, social, manufactured, and financial capital. Discuss how the budget of your campus, community, or country would have to change to reflect all assets.

The David Suzuki Foundation has developed an action plan, called Sustainability Within a Generation, to put Canada on a true path to sustainability by the year 2030. It proposes:

*Improving efficiency:* Over ninety percent of material used in manufacturing becomes waste. We can reduce waste by applying efficiency standards to appliances, passenger vehicles, homes, and commercial buildings. Shifting to renewable energy sources like wind, solar, and micro-hydro would also help us achieve this goal.

*Eliminating waste and pollution:* Eliminating waste means designing production and consumption processes and patterns so waste is not created. In addition to limiting environmental impacts, reducing waste can enhance economic opportunities, create jobs, and save money.

*Building sustainable cities:* We can promote regional and national planning that integrates transportation, land-use, and environmental planning; and ensures municipal infrastructure is sustainable and based on smart growth. It's also important to put an end to urban sprawl, which causes air pollution, water pollution, habitat destruction, gridlock, and loss of productive farmland.

# Economics and Consumption

As the title of this book insists, sustainability must be considered in the context of social well-being and economic fairness, as well as environmental factors. Otherwise, solutions run the risk of being inherently unsustainable. This makes teaching sustainability that much more complex and challenging. Teachers and others must broaden their understanding of these subjects in order to best help others learn about them.

## 21. Explore a Living Economy

We study living systems in nature, but how does this apply to human creations and institutions? Solicit ideas on what would constitute a "living economy" and how our current system meets or falls short of such features.

Visit the web site of the Business Alliance for Local Living Economies at www.livingeconomies.org for inspiration. Also see David C. Korten's essay "Living Economies for a Living Planet." He writes, "A living economy is comprised of fair-profit [in contrast to profit maximizing] and not-for-profit living enterprises that are place-based, human-scale, stakeholder-owned, democratically accountable, and life-serving. In contrast to the publicly-traded, limited-liability corporation, which is best described as a pool of money dedicated to its self-replication, living enterprises function as communities of people engaged in the business of creating just, sustainable, and fulfilling livelihoods for themselves while contributing to the economic health and prosperity of the community" (Korten 2002). What would it look like for your community to be a living economy?

## 22. Use an Ecological Measure of Consumption

Explore the various uses of the Ecological Footprint with your classes or other groups.

A forest health expert describes one approach: "Most students—and most individuals living in industrialized countries—do not make a direct living off natural resources. The environmental consequences of every day actions are buffered in so many ways: air conditioning, central heating, imported food and clothing, insulated buildings, cars, buses, pavement, centralized utilities, etc. The Ecological Footprint (EF) is one of the most concrete, tangible ways for students to measure the impact of their everyday choices and connect those choices to sustainability. The EF is a land area equivalent measure of an individual's consumption and waste generation—the cumulative impact of every day choices. Assign students a semester-long exercise to calculate their EF at the beginning of the course and then make efforts to consciously reduce the footprint throughout the semester. At the end of the semester, ask them to re-calculate their EF and compose a reflection of their experience." See www.rprogress.org/newprojects/ecolFoot.shtml. How does using the EF concept change perceptions of one's everyday activities?

## 23. Change the Cost Paradigm

From teachers and campus administrators to students living on campus or renting nearby, people are involved in the built environment every day. There is a general misconception that using sustainable practices in building projects automatically equates to increased costs. Investigate local projects. Find architects and builders who can make the case for "greener," yet more cost effective, designs.

Brian Dunbar is an architect and Associate Professor in Construction Management who directs a sustainable building group, the Institute for the Built Environment, which helped bring two new "green" design school buildings in on budget. Fossil Ridge High School, for example, was awarded Leadership in Energy and Environmental Design (LEED) silver certification and is now saving the Poudre School District in Fort Collins, CO over one hundred thousand dollars per year in energy costs and uses sixty percent less energy when compared to other modern high schools.

## 24. Show How Sustainability Contributes to Staying "In the Black"

The key to running a successful business is staying profitable. When presenting sustainability-minded projects, lead off with return on investment and economical feasibility.

Traditional business is run with an eye on a single bottom line (financial) as opposed to the "triple bottom line" idea that sustainability represents. Because any good business person realizes the value of staying in the black, anyone presenting sustainability innovations must address the dollars aspect, and is wise to do so first. Simply put, sustainability is about running a profitable business for a long time in an environmentally and socially balanced manner. Ask students to interview local business owners regarding their single and triple bottom lines.

## 25. Understand Synergistic Relationships

Contact your local facilities staff for an analysis of the costs associated with your building and explore how other decisions could have made a big difference. Most of the components necessary to construct a building have synergistic relationships. For example, an upgrade to one building system may entail a cost increase but may result in a cost decrease associated with a related building component.

A leading sustainable building educator notes, "When I talk to students and other audiences, I often refer to the Association of General Contractors Foundation's assessment that buildings in the U.S. account for approximately sixty-five percent of electrical energy consumption, thirty percent of green house gas emissions, thirty percent of raw material usage, thirty percent of waste output, and twelve percent of potable water usage. In the building industry, many sustainable options may be eliminated because of a presumed increase in cost. While sustainable building components may be more expensive than traditional components, they may also result in a cost decrease or measurable benefit to another building component (resulting in a synergistic effect). For example, increasing the thermal resistance of an exterior wall may result in increased construction costs for the wall but may also allow a reduction in the size and cost of heating and cooling devices needed while providing a more comfortable interior space."

## 26. Recognize the Power of Consumers as Agents of Change

Calculate the ecological, economic, and social impact consumers can make through purchasing choices. We positively affect our economy, community, and the natural environment if we are more deliberate with our consumer decisions.

If consumers demanded more products and services that contributed to sustainability, the private sector and government would respond accordingly. Recycling plastic, for example, is not an economically viable option in much of the United States because there is insufficient consumer demand for goods made from recycled plastic. Our choices as consumers drive the economy and our communities and, therefore, the health of the environment. What choices can students make and encourage others to make for a more sustainable community and planet?

## 27. Promote Inclusive Prosperity

Present a case study for a sustainable safety net. Discuss what changes are needed in our culture to create a secure future for all and how the environment can benefit from economic innovation and social stability.

In an analysis of the successes of the Finnish people in crafting government policy that requires heavy taxes but ensures a healthy foundation for ongoing innovation, Peter Ford describes their collective belief: "High level education is the key to what Pekka Himanen, a brilliant young philosopher who advises the Finnish government, calls his country's 'virtuous circle.' 'When people can fulfill their potential, they become innovators…. The innovative economy is competitive and makes it possible to finance the welfare state, which is not just a cost, but a sustainable basis for the economy, producing new innovators with social protection.' In the end, says Jorma Sipila, the Chancellor of Tampere University, Finland's inclusive social model is its best guarantee for the future. 'The conditions for a flourishing economy are so demanding that the state has to make social investments to raise competent people and take care of dropouts so that they carry their share of the burden.'... Marrying prosperity and social protection is the only sustainable future" (Ford 2005, 6–7). How can other governments follow the lead of the Finnish?

## 28. Pick Low-Hanging Fruit First

Small efforts can pay off in big ways. List a few small but immediate goals that would begin moving your class or organization toward sustainability.

Consider practical applications of oncologist Karl-Henrik Robèrts' *Natural Step* framework for sustainability in business. One of Dr. Robèrts' messages is to incorporate small sustainable changes that pay off in the short-term and then build upon them in a step-by-step manner, "picking the low hanging fruit" first. For example, in schools and colleges, teachers can assign students a semester-long project to identify a problem on their campus or within the community, propose and institute a solution, and present their accomplishments. The key to getting off to a successful start is to define a clear focus and take on a manageable issue. It has to be something that will cost the institution little or nothing to fix and can be accomplished within a semester.

## 29. Address Disparities

Discuss the enduring inequities that undermine movement toward a more sustainable future.

In *No Future Without Forgiveness*, Bishop Desmond Tutu recognizes the threats to healing in post-apartheid South Africa when serious attention is not paid to the enduring privileges of so many in the minority white community when contrasted with the persistent poverty of so many in the majority black community: "In South Africa the whole process of reconciliation has been placed in very considerable jeopardy by the enormous disparities between the rich, mainly the whites, and the poor, mainly the blacks. The huge gap between the haves and the have-nots, which was largely created and maintained by racism and apartheid, poses the greatest threat to reconciliation and stability in our country.... For unless houses replace the hovels and shacks in which most blacks live, unless blacks gain access to clean water, electricity, affordable health care, decent education, good jobs, and a safe environment—things which the vast majority of whites have taken for granted for so long—we can just as well kiss reconciliation goodbye" (Tutu 1999, 273–274). Brainstorm a list of inequities in your own culture and how they prevent sustainability on all levels.

# 30. Compare Needs With Wants

Many people in the developed world want—and have—much more than they need. Advertising feeds these wants in order to increase corporate profits. Have people reflect on their own needs and wants within a context of sustainability.

A disposable consumer society is like a never-ending conveyer belt of the latest and greatest, with the old and supposedly useless being tossed aside, contributing to the already overflowing level of waste. Historically our necessities meant air, water, food, and protection (from the elements). However, developed societies have created a fifth need, fed by advertising—the need for novelty (Ewen 1986). The American public seems to have been conditioned to expect new products each year in the pursuit of better living. What is behind this need? What factors make it unsustainable? Should it be addressed and, if so, how?

# 31. Explore Community-Based Social Marketing

Students, coworkers and family members can create sustainable programs using Community-Based Social Marketing (CBSM) methods. Doug McKenzie-Mohr and William Smith discuss the profound effectiveness of CBSM in their 1999 book, *Fostering Sustainable Behavior: An Introduction to Community-Based Social Marketing*. They write, "This approach involves: identifying barriers and benefits to a sustainable behavior, designing a strategy that utilizes behavior change tools, piloting strategy with a small segment of a community, and finally, evaluating the impact of the program once it has been implemented across a community" (McKenzie-Mohr 1999, 15). Additional information about CBSM and live projects happening around the world can be found at www.cbsm.com.

The beauty of CBSM is that it is not limited to a certain group of people or type of behavior. Businesses, non-profits, teachers, and local, city, and state governments can use it to create a more responsible citizenry. Assign each student one entity with which to try this approach.

# Design, Nature, and Buildings

Think about our built environment, where designs too often prioritize views or orientation to the street over the southern exposures needed to maximize thermal benefits from the sun. Huge HVAC systems are commonly installed to compensate for inefficient vaulted ceilings. As David Orr argues in *Earth in Mind*, architecture reflects our values; self-indulgence, convenience, mass-production, and faddish design take precedence over energy conservation. It is not surprising that studies show access to fresh air and natural lighting boosts the morale of teachers and students alike. Pushing for renovations and new buildings to adhere to "green" principles can be a catalyst for important discussions about sustainability within schools, companies, organizations, families, and communities.

## 32. See Nature as a Mentor

Flip scarcity thinking on its head and focus on the wealth embodied in the natural world. Contemplate the acorn that knows how to be a tree, the salmon that knows its way home, the butterfly that migrates thousands of miles, and all the green plants that "eat" the sun. What lessons from the natural world can you bring into discussions about sustainability in your class or organization?

In *Biomimicry*, Janine Benyus writes, "[We] can make a conscious choice to follow nature's lead in living our lives. The good news is that we'll have plenty of help: we are surrounded by geniuses. They are everywhere with us, breathing the same air, drinking the same round river of water, moving on limbs built from the same blood and bone. Learning from them will take only stillness on our part, a quieting of the voices of our own cleverness. Into this quiet will come a cacophony of earthly sounds, a symphony of good sense" (Benyus 1997, 297).

## 33. Build on Nature's Lead

What if humans built cities like coral reefs that beautifully produced oxygen, sequestered carbon, and improved life for all species? Architect William McDonough (*Cradle to Cradle*) sees nature's laws (photosynthesis, self-assembly, etc.) as magic and as models for rethinking our built environments.

Take a tour of your campus or town. What buildings embody some of this natural wisdom?

## 34. Remember the Pen Is Mightier Than the Sword, but the Wrench Is Mightier Still

Connect people with those who hold the tools needed for sustainability, who can help redesign engines and buildings or grow foods without chemical pesticides or fertilizers. These skilled innovators hold real tools for sustainability and can help transform our system.

Workshops and programs that address sustainable living skills are offered around the country. The annual Rocky Mountain Sustainable Living Fair in Fort Collins, CO (see www.sustainablelivingfair.org) is one of many events where citizens can meet people who produce biodiesel, build sustainable structures, and install photovoltaic solar panels. Have students investigate human resources in the community.

## 35. Understand How Classrooms Can Teach

David Orr, in *Earth in Mind*, uses the phrase "architecture as pedagogy" to describe the fact that we learn *from* buildings, not just in them. Many of today's educational buildings teach students that locality is unimportant, energy can be squandered, and disconnectedness is normal. Although many of us spend ninety percent of our time indoors, few understand how buildings actually work, let alone their full effects on our health, psyche, and the natural environment. Make an inventory of what your buildings teach.

On the faculty in environmental studies at Oberlin, Katy Janda observes, "The lessons we learn from architecture are usually tacit rather than explicit, and few people other than architects are ever taught to read the language of the built environment. As a result, the general population tends to treat buildings as static objects rather than dynamic systems. Developing a higher level of building literacy articulates the lessons absorbed from existing buildings and, concurrently, provides a basis for understanding the need for change." Katy recommends the following exercise: "An infrared thermometer (also known as a 'spot pyranometer') enables the user to point a laser at a building component or material and measure its surface temperature. This device can be used as a proxy for an infrared camera by superimposing a grid on a surface and taking a number of readings. By using the infrared thermometer to make invisible flows of energy visible, students are able to compare the effectiveness of their classroom's windows and walls at retaining heat (or cold, depending on the season). This exercise can be expanded in various ways to demonstrate concepts of heat flow in series and in parallel, and has been used to add elements of sustainability to several different high school subjects, including geometry, remedial math, and home economics."

# 36. Reframe Conventional Design

Identify the ways in which more sustainable designs in your buildings would be a benefit. Issues in design are often framed in ways that make sustainability seem burdensome. These misinterpretations are rooted in supposed deficiencies of conventional design and should be presented as such.

Present these challenges for what they really are—issues in water use, climate change, energy, natural resource use, consumption, and related social issues. Offer sustainable design as the *solution set* to these "issues." By focusing on the solution set, people become empowered and stay more positive, two critical conditions for learning. By presenting them as issues or challenges in conventional design, students are much more likely to be open to new ideas and see the solution set emanating from sustainable design. Explore, for example, the building in which your class meets. What are the issues of design involved? How can sustainable practices be used as a solution set to address these issues?

# 37. Create Spaces That Love You Back

Whether retrofitting an existing space or designing a new one, think of it as a living space, one that you would want to be in whether working or not. Add other aspects of a friendly work environment, such as warming colors, shapes, and textures that are pleasing to the senses, artistic expression, and ample space for sharing/preparing food, and you have a work space that loves you back. The end result is happier workers, students, teachers, and families.

At New Belgium Brewing Company there are a variety of different work-spaces. Many people work in production areas like the warehouse, packaging hall, brewhouses, and fermentation cellar, while others work at their desks for areas like engineering, finance and accounting, marketing, and IT. Yet, these spaces are all occupied by people. One staff member reports, "Studies have shown that people are happier when they are exposed to sunlight and have access to a view while they work, whether at school, in a place of business, or at home. With this in mind, New Belgium has worked to incorporate natural daylight into areas of the brewery where applicable, office spaces filled with various colors and textures made mostly from recycled goods, an open and accessible kitchen, and meeting spaces that contain color and art scattered about the facility. Many people who work at the brewery enjoy their jobs not just because of what they do, but also because of where they work." Ask students what they like and don't like about their living and working spaces. What would they change?

# 38. "Leed" by Example

Use the LEED rating system developed by the U.S. Green Building Council (USGBC) to introduce people to their built environment. The USGBC created LEED to promote sustainability and guide green building practices among design and construction professions, but it is valuable for any audience that needs to understand the relationships between land, resources, and the buildings we inhabit.

Since its inception in 2000, the LEED system has been applied to a growing number of projects and its use is mandated by many states, cities, universities, and school districts. One Construction Management instructor describes a class exercise: "Using the LEED scorecard (printable from www.usgbc.org) as a handout, I guided students through the LEED categories of site, water, energy, materials, and indoor environmental quality. I asked them to imagine a particular building project or a classroom remodel. In groups, they first visualized and then discussed how the LEED requirements could be integrated. This exercise allowed them to think about the specific impacts these projects have because of their design and resource utilization." Invite an architect or facilities staff member into your class or meeting to evaluate your room and building with respect to LEED or "green" criteria.

# 39. Seek Out Buildings That Allow Students to Teach

Identify buildings in your area that could serve as instructive laboratories for studying the relationship between design and energy use.

From an educational standpoint, the building that houses Bacon Elementary School in Fort Collins, CO is a gem. As soon as this environmentally friendly school opened in 2003, students who participate in its Explorers LAB (Learning Above and Beyond) began to study the building's design, energy consumption, and use of renewable versus nonrenewable sources of energy. They learned how designing a smart building can conserve both energy and dollars every day. A fifth grade teacher, Dianne Odbert, organized a team of Student Ambassadors for Environmental Stewardship. At the dedication of the school, they described the process for an audience of about 500. Over the years, these student ambassadors have given tours to many other students as well as various community groups. According to Odbert, "It is one thing to talk about environmental stewardship and energy conservation. The lesson goes a whole lot further when students are essentially handed their entire school and empowered to learn and teach from it." Ask students to find "educational" buildings in their own surroundings.

# 40. View Biology Through a New Lens

*Biomimicry* is a new term for emulating nature's survival strategies in the design of human products and systems. It is also a stimulating method for presenting biology to people of all ages.

Ask people to choose items they have with them—combs, backpacks, jackets, hats, keys, and so forth—and identify what purpose each item serves. Then give them time to come up with examples from the biological world that perform these same functions. For example, when they choose a jacket, they discover that hair, fur, and feathers perform similarly. Spend time discussing how these natural materials were produced, contrasted with the process used to create the personal items. Viewing biology through this "functional lens" allows people to see, often for the first time, the inherent sustainability found in nature.

# Ethics, Values, and the Sacred

Sustainability is more than how we think about the environment, our societies, and economies; it is deeper than becoming more conscious of our daily activities. It is important to recognize the ethical base that reflects our values and underlies our thoughts and actions. For many, sustainability also incorporates an important sacred or spiritual dimension.

## 41. Rethink Basic Rights

History will judge everyone harshly—especially our educators—if too few are willing to respond to the threats to maintaining a sustainable, collective existence. Examine the basic assumptions in your own field for barriers to greater environmental responsibility, societal well-being, and economic fairness. Allow your conclusions to be a starting point for discussion.

Winona LaDuke, Native American author, activist, and one-time Green Party candidate for vice president, has written about the need for a "seventh generation" constitutional amendment to protect our common property. Such an amendment would inject an intergenerational perspective concerning oceans, air, forests, rivers, water, and public lands into our policies and practices. Explore the virtues and shortcomings of a culture based on private property or common property or a combination of both, and how each impacts sustainability. How do such matters mesh or conflict with our notions of capitalism, property, democracy, and so forth?

# 42. Nurture an Ethic for Nature

Identify opportunities to meet outdoors where people can experience nature firsthand. Such experiences can be important for the development of an ethic that values sustainability.

Consider this passage from Aldo Leopold's classic *A Sand County Almanac:* "The Golden Rule tries to integrate the individual to society, democracy to integrate social organization to the individual. There is as yet no ethic dealing with man's relation to land and to the animals and plants which grow upon it. Land, like Odysseus' slave-girls, is still property. The land relation is still strictly economic, entailing privileges but no obligations" (Leopold 1949, 244). There is a direct and positive correlation between time spent in the natural environment and the strength of one's ethic toward nature. Get outside; challenge your students to think about how they are asked and expected to treat others. Then ask them to consider how we treat the natural environment. Being outside can help students think through such an issue with greater clarity and intellect.

# 43. Explore What Informs Revered Leaders

Research the life stories and writings of Nobel Peace Prize winners, spiritual thinkers, and visionary leaders. Discuss what themes in their thinking speak to the sustainability of the web of life. Here are two inspirations:

*From Martin Luther King Jr.*, referring to the human species: "All persons are caught in an inescapable network of mutuality, tied to a single garment of destiny. What affects one directly, affects all indirectly" (King 1963).

*From Vietnamese Buddhist monk*, Thich Nhat Hanh, who was nominated for the Nobel Peace Prize by Martin Luther King, Jr., "Imagine a circle with its center point 'C.' The circle is composed of all the points equidistant from C. The circle is there because all the points are there. If even one point is missing, the circle immediately disappears. The presence of one point of the circle depends on the presence of all the other points.... Here too we see that

'One is all, all is one,' every point of the circle is of equal importance…. Each is vital to the existence of the whole and therefore to the existence of all the other parts. This is interdependence" (Hanh 1988, 69).

# 44. Align Values and Actions

Ask students to complete the statement, "I would be happier if _____."
Compile the results to create a basis for discussing, within a context of sustainability, how they spend their time and resources.

Brett Bruyere teaches classes on the environment. It has been his experience that "most individuals will complete the above sentence with a value related to family, friends, spirituality or some such intangible. Yet our society is awash with advertising that insinuates that happiness can be achieved by owning the latest electronic gear, wearing a certain clothing style, driving a new car, drinking a certain beer, or living in a bigger house. Credit card debt and bankruptcy filings were at their highest levels in history in 2004-2005, hardly a recipe for happiness." Bruyere adds that his own students often "feel empowered to change their own behavior when they realize that some of their consumption fails to contribute significantly to their personal happiness in life." Ask students to identify three areas of their own life that don't contribute to their own, or Earth's, happiness.

# 45. See Enemies as Potential Allies

Accepting the world the way it is may block us from seeing other and better ways forward. Use role-plays with students or groups to surface polarized positions, but then emphasize listening, empathy, and negotiation to find common and sustainable ways to move forward.

In *No Future Without Forgiveness*, Nobel Peace Prize recipient Bishop Desmond Tutu describes the emergence of South Africa from the horrors of its brutal system of white minority rule: "The first democratically elected government of South Africa was a government of National Unity made up of members of political parties that were engaged in a life-and-death struggle. The man who headed it had been incarcerated for twenty-seven years as a dangerous terrorist. If it could happen there, surely it can happen in other places. Perhaps God chose such an unlikely place deliberately to show the world that it can be done anywhere" (Tutu 1999, 280).

# 46. Plant Hope

Pass along reports of ingenuity that rally the human spirit. Find stories that celebrate creative and constructive responses to the "doom and gloom" reports of environmental, societal, and economic decline.

Looking down on the glitter of Brazil's Rio de Janeiro are the inhabitants of slums *(flavelas)* that cover the hillsides. Here, enterprising American students from Temple University have begun hydroponic vegetable gardens to demonstrate inexpensive rooftop solutions to the problem of a lack of locally grown fresh produce. As reporter Marion Lloyd notes, "Although hydroponics does not work for root vegetables and trees, which require soil and space, the system is ideal for growing a wide variety of plants like tomatoes and beans.... The students are working with a local nongovernmental organization, Viva Rio, which directs dozens of development programs in the flavelas.... The system is extremely lightweight and portable—a must for slum residents, who are constantly in the process of building new floors onto their houses as they can afford to. It can also be hung from balconies, and requires less water than conventional soil gardens. And the produce not only grows more quickly—a head of lettuce takes a month to mature, instead of the usual six weeks—but also doesn't require pesticides" (Lloyd 2005, A56). Ask students to research other sustainable inventions.

# 47. Use Precaution as Wisdom

Encourage open and honest dialogue about *what we don't know*, and how we can proceed when consequences of our actions, innovations, or technologies are unpredictable. Present the *precautionary principle*, the idea that if the consequences of an action are unknown, but are judged to have some potential for major or irreversible negative consequences, then it is better to avoid that action.

Author Carolyn Raffensperger states, "An elegant door leading out of the maze is the precautionary principle, the simple notion of forecaring.... We can give the benefit of the doubt to the Earth rather than to profits. We can set goals for the kind of world we want to live in.... The precautionary principle gets us out of the maze and puts us on a path of restraint and ecological wisdom. A path of reverence" (Raffensperger 2005, 4). Research the place of the Precautionary Principle and its application to your field, to political decision making, and to personal, collective, and environmental health. What are the effects of thinking first of future generations before permitting something genetically engineered, radioactive, or containing untested chemicals to be used?

## 48. Acknowledge Grief, Invite Connection

We live in times of loss—loss of species, loss of cultures, and loss of languages. Introducing rituals for acknowledging the associated grief can help release energy for new, sustainable commitments.

In *The Ecology of Commerce*, Paul Hawken writes, "At the present rate of extinction—estimates range from 20,000 to over 100,000 species every year…the loss of evolutionary potential is being called the 'death of birth.' This is tantamount to marching backward through the Cenozoic Are, losing millions of years of evolutionary development in a matter of decades" (Hawken 1993, 29). Some exercises you can use are as follows: Sit in a circle. Light a candle. Play nourishing music. Create a center hearth for photos, words, prayers, stones, and mementoes. Pass a "talking stick" to help hearts speak one by one as others only listen. Speak of grief. Speak of joy. Speak of fear. Speak of love. If culturally appropriate, practice eye contact. Encourage genuine emotion. Invite honesty with kindness. Honor silence. End by sharing food, smiles, and gratefulness. Think of one resource in the area that has been lost and perform a grief ceremony for it.

## 49. Brainstorm a "Should" List

Examine the ethical codes or standards that exist for your professional association, business, or other organization. Discuss the rationale for those ideals, and how they must have developed through collaboration and consensus-building within your profession. Then, with your students, or others, examine the code of ethics and improve it using appropriate behavior based on sustainable principles.

In his book *In Accord with Nature*, Clifford Knapp suggests first asking people to compile their own individual lists of how humans should act when it comes to sustainability. Compile all of these individual lists and challenge your class or group to create a consensus code of ethics. Good facilitation is key; most people will agree on some points but may have difficulty with others. (See www.ethicsweb.ca/codes/ for tips on how to write a code of ethics.)

# 50. Find Ways to Use Faith

Identify religious allies. Find inspiration in the collective ideas and actions of Judeo-Christian, Muslim, Buddhist, and indigenous peoples and others actively pursuing sustainability or the "triple bottom line" of environmental, economic, and societal health.

In a paper offered to the United Nations Millennium Peace Summit, entitled *Ecumenical Witness For Peace, Justice & Sustainability*, the National Council of Churches USA (representing fifty-two million members of one hundred forty thousand congregations) affirmed this vision (National Council of Churches USA 2000):

- Responsible participation in civil life
- Economic well-being and social health for all
- Oneness and mutuality of the human family
- Doing justice, loving neighbors near and far
- Universal peace and reconciliation
- Human dignity and rights
- Care for creation and conservation of natural resources

What are faith-based groups doing in your community and beyond?

# 51. Read Sacred Texts

See what you can discover by reading sacred texts in the light of sustainability.

For clear communication, it is important to share a common language and also to understand the underpinnings of what others value and believe. For example, the Bible has helped to shape thinking for many in the United States and elsewhere about the environment, the economy, and human relationships. Reading sacred texts can provide insight into these roots. Discuss your findings with family, friends, students, and others.

# Personal Responsibility and Empowerment

We can only accomplish so much by looking for answers from politicians and community leaders. We must also address the individual's role in promoting more sustainable practices and rallying support for needed reforms.

## 52. Understand the Tipping Point

Analyze major political changes like women's suffrage and the civil rights movement to better understand what constitutes the "tipping point" when enough people come together that long and sustained effort can be put forth to create change.

In *The Tipping Point*, Malcom Gladwell describes how decades, if not longer, were required to garner the critical mass of public support to achieve many of the United States' greatest successes. Review the history that led to events like the passage of the Civil Rights Act to understand how such a milestone was the culmination of decades of contributions toward the movement. Students and others will begin to understand that major shifts in societal behavior and values require a mass of people to reach a particular point after which the desired changes become gradually accepted as the norm. Discuss the extent to which each of us is contributing to the tipping point of sustainability.

## 53. Realize That Objects in the Mirror Are More Important Than They Appear

Ask students, colleagues, friends, and others to contemplate a daily routine—such as reading the newspaper or driving across town on an errand—and list the sustainable and unsustainable aspects of that routine. Then direct them to consider alternative and more environmentally, economically, and socially friendly ways to satisfy the same routine and list the potential consequences of the routine changes.

In their thought-provoking book, *Stuff: The Secret Life of Everyday Things*, John Ryan and Alan Durning ponder the consequences of daily tasks. Students are often eager to share their reflections and conclusions, triggering a lively and entertaining interchange. This "mirror" exercise takes only five to ten minutes of individual reflection time, yet yields a wealth of topics, ideas, sharing, and potentially new levels of thinking about personal sustainability.

## 54. Aim to Inspire

Provide images of solutions to social and environmental challenges.

An award-winning consultant on renewable energy told us, "When I talk to people about solar energy, I often find that they think there is only one technology. Showing pictures of a variety of applications broadens their understanding of what can be done. Ask a group to find images depicting new solutions to environmental challenges. Have someone arrange the images on a class web site or a poster so the abundance of ideas is apparent and inspiring. Now move beyond reality by asking the group to imagine solutions for which the technology may not yet exist."

## 55. Loosen Up on Expectations

Beware of setting goals that limit what others can learn. Letting go of rigid expectations can leave you open to seeing a variety of unexpected results.

While guiding tours at New Belgium Brewing Company, Allison Aichinger has enjoyed seeing her environmental advocacy evolve: "Initially I wanted our tour guests to walk away full of inspiration from New Belgium's environmental efforts. I now see that without being tied to the outcome of my tours, I am planting more seeds of environmental consciousness. I sprinkle my tour with references to big concepts like zero waste, the triple bottom line and closing waste loops—these are key phrases that people can Google on their own time if they feel a resonance with the topic. Often these ideas are completely new to people, so providing a real time example is important. When I explain how New Belgium's process water treatment plant has allowed us to capture and utilize methane gas as an energy source, guests understand and get a clear picture in their minds of a waste loop closing. People are often floored by these simple connections." What unexpected results have you, your students, colleagues, family members, and others seen in your sustainability work already?

# 56. Remember to Save the Humans

Engage in open dialogue about the role of humans on the planet. Realize that our need to "save the environment" is grounded in self-preservation as much as it is in respect for all things nonhuman.

A local sustainability advocate reflects: "When I first entered college I was all about saving the whales. I felt humans were a horrible cancer on this earth, and that we would destroy this planet without ever knowing the beauty it really held. After my experiences in college, I realized it was not about saving what is around us, but rather about changing human behavior to be less destructive of what is around us. It was all about saving the humans. Every choice we make has an impact on the plants and animals (including we humans) on this planet. With this in mind, you can make more choices based on respect for what is around you." How does a change in focus from saving the planet to saving the humans impact your group's efforts?

# 57. Identify New Leaders

Given the changes needed for a more sustainable future that balances environmental, economic, and societal needs, we need to find leaders who will spearhead these changes. Make a list of individuals who could lead this redirection. Identify leaders from the past who had the qualities needed today.

In *Enough: Staying Human in an Engineered Age,* Bill McKibben identifies Gandhi as someone who is widely revered for challenging the world to use nonviolent noncooperation as a mechanism for resistance to powerful oppressors. Yet Gandhi also represented much more. "It is no coincidence that Gandhi was also the most powerful twentieth-century spokesman for the proposition that less is more, that human satisfaction lies in respecting material limits, in opening yourself to the claims of others, in backing away from the hyperindividualism of the West" (McKibben 2003, 217). Are there any leaders who support sustainability already in place in your community?

## 58. Write the President

Encourage students, colleagues, and others to take stands on issues related to sustainability and submit written commentaries to a local newspaper's opinion section. You can be helpful in assisting them to communicate in a clear and persuasive manner.

Peter Newman, an assistant professor of natural resource management, reports: "As a student, I had the privilege to meet David Brower, ex-director of the Sierra Club, creator of Friends of the Earth, and environmental 'archdruid.' At the time I was working for Yosemite Institute and asked Mr. Brower what message I should give my students each week. With a stern look and a grumpy demeanor he said, 'Tell them to write the President,' and he walked away. I had expected a longer, more complex message. What I realized was that his accomplishments over a lifetime of work were not built on esoteric lectures, but rather on a commitment to deliberate action. I now pass this message on to my own students."

## 59. Pause and Reflect, but Keep Moving

Take a few minutes to write down the progress you have already made in promoting sustainability at work and in your own life. Now list three to five short- and long-term goals.

At the end of his autobiography, Nelson Mandela offers the following reflection: "I have walked that long road to freedom. I have tried not to falter; I have made missteps along the way. But I have discovered the secret that after climbing a great hill, one only finds that there are many more hills to climb. I have taken a moment here to rest, to steal a view of that glorious vista that surrounds me, to look back on the distance I have come. But I can only rest for a moment, for with freedom come responsibilities, and I dare not linger, for my long walk is not yet ended" (Mandela 1994, 625).

# *Plan Ahead*

Reducing waste, restoring the environment, and promoting community well-being and economic health requires teaching new concepts and skills for students of all kinds. Careful planning is essential; you should also look beyond the established curriculum for other fresh, innovative strategies.

## 60. Think About Your Goals

Take time to reflect on your teaching practices; consider the environmental, economic, and social changes that have occurred in the past few years. Make a list of changes to implement in the design and delivery of your material.

As increases in population, industrial production, and waste take an increasing toll on people and the planet, we must find ways to change our course content and approaches to instruction. Consider how you can incorporate sustainable practices into teaching about sustainability. For example, practice recycling (environmental); consider the impact on the budgets of your students of required classroom supplies (economic); and be sure to include all classroom voices in every discussion (social).

## 61. Remember There's More to Education

List the purposes of your own classes or presentations. Identify what is basic information and what goes beyond the basic and speaks to bigger, life supporting issues.

In *Happiness and Education*, Stanford's Nel Noddings questions the traditional goals of education: "It is as though our society has simply decided that the purpose of schooling is economic—to improve the financial condition of individuals and to advance the prosperity of the nation. Hence, students should do well on standardized tests, get into good colleges, obtain well-paying jobs, and buy lots of things. Surely there is more to education than this" (Noddings 2003, 4). In a similar way, we could question the purpose of presentations that only offer basic information and ignore opportunities to challenge and inspire. Take some time to think about how your instruction teaches students how to be more than just consumers.

# 62. Take Advantage of Technology

Technology is making the world smaller and more connected. You can use the internet, new equipment, and various computer programs to bring students and others closer to authors, innovators, and leaders promoting sustainability.

Many schools, colleges, universities, organizations, and businesses have the resources to link people locally with important contacts at different sites around the world using the internet, Voice Over Internet Protocols (VOIP), and video conferences. These technologies can be used to beam authors, researchers, and other sources directly into classes. Students often hold these people up on a pedestal. By interacting directly with them, students are often inspired to join an active and influential community that is dedicated to sustainability.

# 63. Bring Your Students on Business Trips…Virtually

Investigate ways to use technology to share your participation in various conferences on sustainability with your students, colleagues, and others back home.

Peter Newman, an Assistant Professor of Protected Area Management, writes, "There have been several times over the last few years that I wish my students could have been flies on the wall at meetings away from campus so I could point out the real world context for the theories and practices we were studying in class. In 2003, the World Parks Congress was held in South Africa. The congress brought together world leaders in Parks and Protected Areas Management as well as historical figures such as Nelson Mandella and Queen Noor of Jordan. The meeting lasted two weeks. During that time I set up a web site that enabled students to read, see pictures of, and even listen to selected talks at the congress. Each day I wrote a blog that discussed my impressions on meetings with people from all over the world. My students back home responded each day with questions and comments. I even asked several of their questions in sessions and became their voice at the congress. My class had one hundred students and, during my time in South Africa, the course web site logged over one thousand hits from them. They remained very interested in the topic and felt represented." (See www.myclimate.org/EN for one of several avenues to carbon offsetting and reducing greenhouse gas emissions generated from travel.)

# 64. Choose Texts Carefully

Selecting course texts is one of the most important decisions an instructor makes. It may be possible to choose books that cover traditional course material and integrate ideas about sustainability. If not, find ways to supplement course readings. Allow students to suggest resources.

David Gunderson reports that in Advanced Construction Systems, a course that focuses primarily on commercial construction systems, he has "been able to select a text that integrates information on sustainable materials and methods into each chapter." D. Royce, in *Teaching Tips for College and University Instructors: A Practical Guide*, provided questions for him to ask when choosing his texts (Royce 2001, 37):

- Is the material pertinent to course objectives?
- Is the content up to date?
- Is the book organized and logical?
- Is it clearly written?
- Will students find the book interesting and accessible?
- Does it conform to general departmental or professional standards?
- Will students find its cost reasonable?
- Is this book well suited for the way I teach?
- Is this book/edition available in time for the start of class?
- Is there a test bank or instructor's manual available?

Gunderson adds: "I now have another question I want to add to this list: What additional information should be provided to students to supplement any of my texts? Choosing the texts and materials that I use sends a very clear message to students about the values I hold for this field." Like sustainability itself, teaching sustainability should be holistic.

# *Approaches and Assessments*

Many instructors and presenters are hesitant to venture far from the lecture format because they are so wedded to covering specific content. Accordingly, they limit what their students and audiences experience. Traditional large group testing through multiple choice questions also drives instruction toward knowledge acquisition, while higher order thinking is more appropriately assessed through written papers, projects, or presentations. Employing some variety—debates, film clips, guest speakers, simulations, field trips— can help sustain the attention of audiences beyond their role as listeners; they can be active, interactive, and observant evaluators, negotiators, role players, debaters, explorers, and more.

## 65. Explore Multiple Approaches to Powerful Ideas

Some concepts are not necessarily "gettable" the first time around. Something like sustainability has many layers of complexity and may need to be rehashed numerous times. Find areas of study that students feel they "get" and challenge them with new ideas. Encourage conversations that bring out multiple viewpoints and help students and others arrive at coherent, well thought-out conclusions.

For instance, ask what it means to be sustainable from different points of view. How would a dog's opinion about sustainability vary from what you would hear from a butterfly, an old oak tree, a bee, or your grandparents? Hopefully, we all begin to notice that the variety of approaches to a powerful idea doesn't diminish its power; it only enhances its depth and application.

## 66. Use Active, Student-Led Exercises

Become experiential. Change your role from educator to facilitator. Give students and other groups an opportunity to direct their own learning about sustainability, to get involved in research. These approaches are especially important when ideas are inherently complex and interdisciplinary.

The ecological dimension of sustainability has its roots in the physical and biological sciences. The National Research Council's report on scientific learning concluded that students learn best from exchanges with each other and by taking control of their own learning. Investigation in groups can be a very effective way to change attitudes and behaviors. Facilitate instances in which you ask individuals to articulate their ideas or challenge others about sustainability. Empower them to answer their own questions, direct their own experiments, and identify their own protocols for how to apply the scientific method.

## 67. Let the Poets Speak

Keep an eye out for expressive writing that stirs hearts and enlivens discussion. Poet Rafael Jesús González writes: "Without respect and reverence for the Earth, without a passionate love of life, there is no reason for ecological concern. As David Hume clearly stated, 'Reason is and ought to be the slave of passions and never pretend to any other office than to serve and obey them.' Our salvation is in loving life and the Earth that births and sustains it passionately and with the whole heart implicitly and explicitly. If this love is absent, reasons and techniques are useless. If we are on the brink of ecological disaster, it is not for lack of cleverness but because our passions have gone wrong, our values distorted, because we do not love life and Earth enough" (Personal Communication).

Look for poetry that can bring great ideas and emotions into your own classes or groups. Great poets have a license to speak in ways that scholars often don't.

This poem was read by Rafael Jesús González at the World Congress of Poets, Tai'an, Shandong Province, China, November, 2005. It is printed here in its entirety with his permission.

## SI NO HABLAMOS

*Si no hablamos para alabar a la Tierra,*
*    es mejor que guardemos silencio.*

*Loa al aire*
*que llena el fuelle del pulmón*
*y alimenta la sangre del corazón;*
*que lleva la luz,*
*el olor de las flores y los mares,*
*los cantos de las aves y el aullido del viento;*
*que conspira con la distancia*
*para hacer azul el monte*

*Loa al fuego*
*que alumbra el día y calienta la noche,*
*cuece nuestro alimento y da ímpetu a*
*nuestra voluntad;*
*que es el corazón de la Tierra, este*
*fragmento de lucero;*
*que quema y purifica por bien o por mal.*

*Loa al agua*
*que hace a los ríos y a los mares;*
*que da sustancia a la nube y a nosotros;*
*que hace verde a los bosques y los campos;*
*que hincha al fruto y envientra nuestro*
*nacer.*

*Loa a la tierra*
*que es el suelo, la montaña, y las piedras;*
*que lleva los bosques y arraiga nuestro sus-*
*tento,*
*que es el jardín y la arena del desierto;*
*que nos forma los huesos y sala los mares,*
*la sangre;*
*que es nuestro hogar y sitio.*

*Si no hablamos en alabanza a la Tierra,*
*    si no cantamos en celebración de la vida,*
*    es mejor que guardemos silencio.*

## IF WE DO NOT SPEAK

*If we do not speak to praise the Earth,*
*    it is best we keep silent.*

*Praise air*
*that fills the bellow of the lung & feeds*
*our heart's blood;*
*that carries light,*
*the smell of flowers & the seas,*
*the songs of birds & the wind's howl;*
*that conspires with distance*
*to make the mountains blue.*

*Praise fire*
*that lights the day & warms the night;*
*that cooks our food & gives motion to*
*our wills;*
*that is the heart of Earth, this fragment*
*of a star;*
*that burns & purifies for good or ill.*

*Praise water*
*that makes the rivers & the seas;*
*that gives substance to the clouds & us;*
*that makes green the forests & the fields;*
*that swells the fruit & wombs our birth.*

*Praise earth*
*that is the ground, the mountain,*
*& the stones;*
*that holds the forests & roots our*
*sustenance;*
*that is the garden & the desert sand;*
*that builds our bones & salts the seas,*
*the blood;*
*that is our home & place.*

*If we do not speak in praise of the Earth,*
*    if we do not sing in celebration of life,*
*    it is best we keep silent.*

# 68. Implement the Ten-Second Lab

Engaging the interest of audiences while lecturing can be a challenge. Keep yourself alert to the needs of students by introducing a variety of feedback mechanisms.

Lecturing is one of the least effective teaching methods for imparting values, engaging interest, or instilling particular skills, all of which are important for learning sustainability. Yet lecturing is often necessary to synthesize and disseminate current information in a class or for a presentation. As one way to keep any presentation engaging, try this variation: Periodically stop and ask your audience a multiple-choice question. A quick show of hands provides immediate feedback on their learning. Having them hold up cards with the letters A through D protects their identity a bit more and may allow for more risk taking. Some instructors are now using a "laser clicker" that is tied into a computer in class and can instantly record, graph, and display responses from the entire class. Decide if "enough" people have gotten the right answer before moving on. You could also have them discuss a question with others nearby and revise their answers, or you might decide to revisit that subject in more detail and try a different explanation. These quick checks on understanding should not take more than ten seconds and will help keep you and your audience better connected.

# 69. Use Guests and Films to Offer Diverse Perspectives

Invite local leaders and activists to provide first-hand perspectives on issues involving sustainability. Create a speaker's panel. Documentaries can also provide different viewpoints and many films dramatize important issues concerning the environment, the economy, and society.

Controversial issues are often portrayed as two sided, black-and-white affairs. In reality, there may be much common ground among the various stakeholders, more than is immediately apparent. Most people want a vibrant economy and community, and a healthy environment. Differences erupt, however, over how these things can be achieved. Speakers can give first-hand accounts of an issue in all its complexity. You can also use clips from both documentary and popular films to represent diverse perspectives and capture the complexities of community challenges. Films like *Erin Brockovich*, *A Civil Action*, *Mindwalk*, *What the Bleep Do We Know*, and *Silkwood* reveal environmental and social harms, address the economics of powerful interests and community resources, and provoke important discussions because they are based on true stories.

# 70. Invent Games and Have a Little Fun

Look for ways to energize discussions about sustainability with some engaging, creative, and fun activities. Inventing games, for example, can provide a fun and unique way for students to learn. Reinventing games like Monopoly, Jeopardy, or Risk can be equally meaningful, challenging, and fulfilling.

A graduate student with experience in a "green building" project shares the following recommendation: "Students can work in groups and agree to share various duties and responsibilities. Each team then develops a theme or concept for its game and develops a project plan that includes an explanation, individual responsibilities, and a schedule. To ensure students are making satisfactory progress throughout the semester, two project progress reports should be scheduled during the last half of the semester. Eventually, the games are played in class, providing a great way to relieve stress at the end of the semester. Students can evaluate each other's games and provide a retrospective evaluation of their own game."

# 71. Put on Your Guide Hat

Imagine that you are leading a group out in nature. How does your teaching change? Being attentive, flexible, creative, and engaging helps connect people with "place," their surroundings—a bedrock principle for teaching sustainability well.

Try some of these hints from local professionals:

- "You have to adapt and be flexible" (Richard Gilliland, Rocky Mountain National Park Guide).

- "Develop ownership for the ideas you are presenting by using local examples of important issues to spark interest and action" (Chris Romero, Community College Biology Teacher).

- "Make real connections with your audience" (Jeff Maugans, Interpretation Supervisor at Rocky Mountain National Park).

# 72. Trust Your Gut

If you feel there is a connection, there is. Allow yourself, your coworkers, and your students to experience this freedom. Encourage them to trust their intuition and to state what they think about sustainability, even if they don't see themselves as "experts." In some ways, they are!

Sustainability is a dynamic, ongoing process. This means that a person who is considered an expert today in the field of sustainability will be a student again in a year or two. This opens up the playing field and allows each of us to be experts. Recognize that we are all entitled to see new connections, create new theories, and express ideas about sustainability. Because everyone is an expert who knows more than someone else does, ask students what they would say about sustainability to those younger and less experienced than themselves, or those older (who may not have had sustainability introduced to them as a concept in school) than themselves.

# 73. Generate New Data

Advances in technology are revealing new sources of data and challenging popular beliefs. Geographic Information Systems (GIS) programs allow for plotting, integrating, organizing, and analyzing data from any number of environmental, health, and demographic sources. E-mail can transfer data quickly and easily, allowing many people from distant locations to help. Ask your students, guests, colleagues, and neighbors to be alert to sources of new data. Better yet, collect new data about a local issue needing attention and explore the various uses of technology for understanding what is happening.

Peter Spotts reports how satellite technology is resolving one debate: "Brazil's Amazon rain forest—one of the most biologically productive regions on the planet—is disappearing twice as fast as scientists previously estimated. That is the stark conclusion ecologist Gregory Asner and his colleagues reached after developing a new way to analyze satellite images to track logging here. The team traces the additional loss to illegal selective logging, which removes trees piecemeal from a forest, rather than carving large swaths. This has made it easier to hide. This project is the first time satellites have been used to track selective logging. For the region, this activity increases the forest's vulnerability to wildfires and undermines its biological productivity. Illegal selective logging in the region releases nearly 100 million tons of additional carbon dioxide into the atmosphere each year" (Spotts 2005, 4). Ask students to explore the interplay between technology and sustainability.

# Learning Through Experience

Only so much can be learned from direct instruction and lectures. While experiential and other field-based assignments can be time consuming and complex to evaluate, they can also provide powerful, memorable bases for self-reflection and new insights. To enhance sustainability learning, find ways to incorporate these activities into your class.

## 74. Experience It!

Begin a lesson about complex sustainability topics with a simple activity that can help provide a foundation of understanding.

Brett Bruyere directs Colorado State University's Environmental Learning Center and Ray Aberle directs the University's Challenge Ropes Course. Each has made extensive use of a wide range of physical activities to illustrate particular concepts, principles, and practices. They write: "A simple exercise in sustainability is to gather a group of people around a rope of sufficient strength to support the communal weight. With each person holding the rope with one hand palm up and the other hand palm down, you can ask them to step backward until they are supporting and being supported by the rope and the others. Ask them to find that tension point where they feel they can be comfortably supported. You can then talk about the role of each person in giving a little (palm down) and taking a little (palm up) so as not to throw off the balance. You will also notice that the circle is dynamic—not static. There is movement, change, and flux, just as there is in our economies, communities, and natural environments. Sustainability is not about staying the same, but about being responsive, active, available, aware, and present to change."

# 75. Connect Learning and Service

An excellent way to appreciate the triple bottom line of environmental, economic, and social concerns is to connect your course content or organization in meaningful ways to an unmet need in the community. Use a community service learning project to embed a meaningful field-based experience into your course or program.

Faculty at Colorado State University have established relationships with local nonprofit organizations like Village Earth in order to enable their students to do activities such as work with Lakota people on the Pine Ridge Reservation in South Dakota. Through this coalition, college students have learned about the different social and economic conditions that impact their work on sustainability. Be certain to work with a knowledgeable community partner and focus on meeting real needs to ensure the project will have lasting positive and sustainable effects on the community. Michael and Julie Bopp's *Recreating the World* is an excellent resource for working with diverse cultures and socioeconomic groups. Well designed service learning projects can create positive changes for the community and rich, new insights about sustainability for students.

# 76. Unravel the Gordian Knot

Simple, but innovative, learning activities involving "physical activity" in the classroom can help students conceptualize the complexity and connectedness of ecosystems with the human world. These activities can also break down classroom barriers and energize students.

In *The Winning Trainer: Winning Ways to Involve People in Learning*, Julius Eitington describes an engaging classroom activity, called the Gordian Knot, that teachers have adapted to get students thinking "systematically" and "sustainably" about life on Earth. The activity works like this: Divide the classroom into groups of approximately fifteen students each, and have each group stand in a circle. Ask each person to select a card from a hat or bowl. Each card lists a species associated with a particular ecosystem along with a picture and brief description. Have students tape one card to their front or back. Next, ask each student to grab the hands of two or more others and create a "Gordian Knot," a tangled mess not unlike the real world. Now have your students untangle themselves, without breaking the connections between the hands. The results are inevitably fun and memorable. Spend time debriefing the activity by soliciting comments about the interdependence of life and the collaboration needed to resolve problems. Discuss how these challenges apply to your work with sustainability. (Variations to this exercise include placing an "outsider" or "expert"—such as an environmental official or scientist—with each group to assess progress, offer feedback, or increase the challenge.)

# 77. Make It Rich and Keep It Wild

Instructors can forget about the very resources that inform their subjects, thereby deadening delivery. Get students and other groups out into the wildness of the real world where the environment is continuously connected in complex ways with society and the economy. Make a list of what could be done to create both richer and wilder experiences.

In *Memory: The Key to Consciousness*, Richard Thompson and Stephen Madigan describe a series of experiments with rats raised in either "rich" environments (in social groups and in cages with exercise wheels, toys, and climbing terrain) or "poor" environments (raised individually in standard laboratory cages). Because the rats in enriched environments developed a thicker cerebral cortex (the physiological base for advanced cognition) as well as more synaptic connections, the popular press made much of the importance of artificially stimulated environments for human infants. Thompson and Madigan, however, reported that wild rats also had more developed brains. The most important conclusion is that both "rich" and "wild" represent complex environments that stimulate brain development. Bare environments and isolated experiences limit learning and development.

## 78. Take That Leap of Faith

Moving toward a more sustainable future can happen if enough people begin moving in the right direction. Challenge your students to take that first step in reducing waste, conserving energy, standing up for fairness, challenging greed, and promoting community.

One instructor regularly uses a Challenge Ropes Course. The infamous "leap of faith" really gets everyone's heart pounding. He writes, "Roped in, students climb a thirty-foot telephone pole, find a way to balance themselves on the top and, when their knees stop knocking, leap toward a trapeze hanging some eight feet or so away. Many grab for their own safety ropes as soon as they jump. Others are too timid in their jump to come very close. Some get a finger or two on the trapeze but not enough to hold on. And a few are able to grab, hold, and swing. Whatever happens, everyone cheers. When we debrief this activity, the connections they find to meeting the challenges in their own lives or about finding more sustainable solutions are direct and useful. What fears do they face and how they are able to climb past them? What supports do they have in place? What are they are able to learn from each attempt?" With or without a ropes experience, ask students to evaluate their fears and challenges regarding learning, teaching, and living sustainability.

## 79. Question Assumptions

Awareness activities can provide reference points for important sustainability concepts. Building awareness can begin with simple games that help initiate discussion and clarify key points about sustainability.

Education professor Bill Timpson wanted to prompt new insights with his first-year students. With a large number of balls and other objects in a hula-hoop in the middle, he divided the eighteen students into four teams and announced that the object of this game was to get all the resources for the group in the five minutes that were allotted and that stealing was allowed! "The groups exploded into a crazed effort at getting objects from the middle, taking from the other groups while protecting their own," reports Timpson. "Running, grabbing, pulling, wrestling, shouting, and laughing added to the bedlam. Importantly, no one won. During the debriefing, we revisited the game's goals, questioned the assumptions everyone made and discussed other strategies. One that surfaced was to question the assumption about competition and reframe the 'group' as the 'entire group,' not the smaller teams. 'But that wouldn't be any fun,' said one student. 'The competition energized everyone.' What then followed was an even deeper discussion about the assumptions that underlie the ways in which entire cultures operate and the conflicts that seem to inevitably arise." When students experience directly these lessons on unquestioned assumptions, they can better understand the more abstract arguments about cultural values and conflicts. Experiment with similar games that might be possible in your area.

# 80. Focus the Group

Getting groups to work well can be a challenge, especially when complex issues like sustainability demand informed and coordinated action. Know that your use of various experiential activities can be helpful in raising awareness about teamwork.

Have students pair up and face each in one long line with index fingers held out at chest height, fingernails pointing out. Place a "helium stick," a lightweight collapsible tent pole, on top of their fingers. As a group, have them get the pole to the ground. The only rule is that everyone must keep contact with the pole at all times. "Very quickly," said one instructor, "that pole began to rise. We talked through what was happening and tried to find a strategy we all could agree on but that pole quickly rose again. It was very frustrating. Then a student who was majoring in music, very involved with jazz, and disciplined to listen closely to his fellow musicians in rehearsal and performance, suggested that we close our eyes. That did it. We all seemed better able to block out the distractions and focus more intently. Slowly, we got control and the pole began to go down. What a useful lesson in the demands of effective teamwork." Try this activity with your own group or class. Everyone will quickly see the need for finding a coordinated focus.

# 81. Focus on Investigations

John Dewey firmly believed students should explore new concepts through self-directed studies. Generate a list of potential investigations that would get your students or groups into the field to think about the interrelationships of the three dimensions sustainability: the environment, the economy, and society.

While Dewey would applaud these efforts, he would urge us to go further and encourage students to direct their own investigations rather than treating field experiences as rote laboratory exercises. Tim Pearson has his elementary school classes energized with meaningful student-generated investigations that tie into sustainability. He's asked: "How does fertilizer runoff from the municipal golf course or farms affect the health of local streams, rivers, and lakes? What happens to the population of prairie dogs when a new development begins and people want manicured lawns?" Identify possible issues for investigation on your campus or in your community. For example, is the landscaping sustainable? What plants could be removed or introduced to lower water, fertilizer, and pesticide usage?

# 82. Treat the Rest of the World Like Paradise

A travel course is a wonderful way to connect students to sustainability topics. Setting up a travel course in a pristine setting further enhances the importance of our planetary conditions.

The Institute for the Built Environment at Colorado State University offers a ten-day sustainable building course each May. Participants stay in tent cottages at Maho Bay, an eco-tourist camp in the U.S. Virgin Islands. Class is held for three hours in the morning and two hours in the evening. Afternoons provide time for individual study, group hikes, recreation, and field trips. Sustainability reading and journaling are assigned before and during the course, and a group project is assigned for the final five days. The program focuses on a variety of topics:

- Defining sustainability
- The planet's condition
- Sustainable cities
- Developments
- Buildings and materials
- Renewable energy systems
- Indoor air quality
- Sustainable business
- Eco-tourism practices

Enhanced learning and sensitivity occurs through immersion in a tranquil setting. Participants often remark that they learn the importance of treating the rest of the world as if it were paradise. With sustainability concepts discussed each day, even recreational activities such as snorkeling, kayaking, and watching recycled glass blowing take on new levels of meaning. Contact ecotourism destinations listed in web sites like www.peopleandplanet.net and begin to consider how to fuse curriculum, costs, and travel logistics.

# 83. Develop Natural Schoolyards

Students learning from nature at school is so important. Outside areas can be converted to gardens for what once grew locally. Students can see what it is like to grow gourds in the fall, tend the land, observe the wildlife, and participate in the process of nurturing plants and protecting wildlife.

Try making a prairie garden (see www.ohiodnr.com/publications/prairiegarden/default.htm); growing prairie flowers (see www.naturenorth.com/spring/flora/growing/growing1.html); or developing a residential prairie (see www.sustland.umn.edu/topics/index.html).

# The Positive Learning Climate

We know a great deal about the relationship between student morale and learning, how open communication and trust, for example, help to create a supportive environment.

## 84. Support Fair-Weather Learning

Recognize the parallel between the weather outside and the emotional climate in your class. Consider the level of mutual trust, respect, and support expressed and question how much "stormy weather" may be present in the form of unfair judgments and biases.

In *Concepts and Choices for Teaching*, Bill Timpson and Paul Bendel-Simso write, "The most important tool that you have at your disposal as a teacher is the space in which you do your job. Here we are not simply referring to the classroom space with its chairs and desks where you do your thing every few days, but to the environment which you as a teacher create, and into which you project yourself and your personality. The classroom is, as much as anything else, a communicative and social space where student ambitions and teacher expectation meet, and it is your obligation as a teacher to make this meeting a fruitful one" (Timpson and Bendel-Simso 1996, 3). For example, before delving into a potentially "stormy" discussion, you can ask your group to establish a "shelter" (in the form of a code of conduct) so that everyone will feel safe to talk openly, honestly, and respectfully.

# 85. Nurture a Love of Place

Something very important happens when we connect positively with the places where we live, work, study, and visit. Help students make these connections through field trips, service learning, and similar approaches.

One way to deepen an experience outdoors is to use silence. One environmental professional describes her experience: "When I took a job as a Camp Naturalist for a YMCA camp in the mountains of central Arizona, part of my task was to work with all ages at the camp, five to sixteen, and help them shed their shelter of the city for a view from the tree house, so to speak. What started out as a basic activity for the little ones turned into a sound observation tool for all the campers. It began with having them sit, sometimes in a circle, sometimes not, in a place out of doors. I then offered a focus point for observation, such as, 'Try to find all the circles in this place, without moving, using your sight and hearing.' We sat in silence for twenty minutes, maybe longer. Always I was amazed at the circles these kids discovered—everything from the birds calling to each other in a circle to the shape of a flower. Once they were used to observing and felt comfortable with it, I asked them for a focus point, or sat with none at all. Over time the campers expressed to me their love for those classes, taken in silence, out of doors. They were able to get in touch with the fundamental pieces of their surroundings, and felt more connected because of it."

# 86. Practice Acceptance

Pick an issue and list the various arguments, positions, and interests. Have participants assign a grade (A through F) to each argument to show their willingness to accept other viewpoints even when they may not agree. Look for opportunities to connect your discipline to the complex realities of life where the environment, economics, and our social fabric intersect and produce a range of viewpoints. Challenge everyone to go outside their comfort zone in accepting a variety of perspectives.

The research on critical thinking is very clear: we can get better and more creative decisions when we solicit many different viewpoints if—and this is a very big IF—we can handle the attendant challenges. The complex challenges associated with sustainability demand effective communication, the understanding of group dynamics, and knowing how best to navigate the frustrations that inevitably emerge. In her groundbreaking *Leadership and the New Science*, Margaret Wheatley writes, "[Multiple] and varying responses [give] a genuine richness to…observations. An organization rich with many interpretations develops a wiser sense of what is going on and what needs to be done. Such organizations become more intelligent" (Wheatley 2001, 67).

# 87. Face Problems

Nothing can really improve by avoiding problems or denying that they exist. Ultimately in schools, colleges, businesses, and other organizations, morale and productivity inevitably suffer when real issues are left to fester. In contrast, learning how to face issues and take action can boost the climate for any class, group, or organization.

Noam Chomsky is an eminent scholar of linguistics who has an equally substantial following as a critic of American policies and practices. In *Imperial Ambitions*, he identifies inaction as a major barrier to progress: "There is an enormous amount of human suffering and misery, which can be alleviated and overcome…. I can't see how anyone can fail to have an interest in trying to help people become more engaged in thinking about these problems and doing something about them" (Chomsky 2005, 183). Focus on a compelling problem in your community and, with students or others, brainstorm solutions and possible actions.

# 88. Build on Peacemaking

Who are the peacemakers in your community or organization and how do they operate? Use their influence to create a classroom or organizational culture based on the principles of peacemaking. Creating this culture will help you address the challenges of sustainability and the difficult and complex interactions of environmental, economic, and social factors.

Peace scholar Elise Boulding challenges us to consider fundamental cultural changes: "A peace culture maintains a creative balance among bonding, community closeness, and the need for separate spaces. It can be defined as a mosaic of identities, attitudes, beliefs, and patterns that lead people to live nurturingly with one another and the earth itself without the aid of structured power differentials, to deal creatively with their differences, and to share their resources.... It cannot be said that humans are innately peaceful or aggressive. Both capacities are there. It is socialization, the process by which society rears its children and shapes the attitudes and behaviors of its members of all ages, that determines how peacefully or violently individuals and institutions handle the problems that every human community faces in the daily work of maintaining itself" (Boulding 2005, 41). Discuss with students and others how a peace culture is similar to or different from a sustainable culture.

## 89. Go for the "Jazz"

Rethink an upcoming lesson or course design. Build in more opportunities for students to work in teams, learn from each other, and apply what they are learning as they explore the various dimensions of sustainability. In *Leadership and the New Science*, Margaret Wheatley draws parallels between the organization of the natural world and what works best with humans. Making music together, especially jazz, offers a useful metaphor: "This world demands that we be present together, and be willing to improvise. We agree on the melody, tempo, and key, and then we play. We listen carefully, we communicate constantly, and suddenly there is music, possibilities beyond anything we imagined. The music comes from somewhere else, from a unified whole we have accessed among ourselves, a relationship that transcends our false sense of separateness. When the music appears, we can't help but be amazed and grateful" (Wheatley 2001, 45).

Have students discuss how this music making appears in working toward sustainability.

## 90. Look Ahead With Hope

Frame discussions about the future with hope and belief in the human ability to solve problems. Be hopeful and realistic. Encourage students and other audiences to play their parts in building a supportive community.

Scientists at a prestigious university once predicted environmental disaster if widespread changes did not occur. A U.S. presidential commission once forecasted super-plagues and mass starvation by the year 2000. While certain diseases like AIDS are devastating and many in the world go hungry, the world has not ended as some have predicted. Forecasting the future is difficult; human beings are too unpredictable and their ingenuity has surpassed what most previous generations thought possible. When discussing the future, be hopeful and honest. Consider how problems could be solved realistically. Ask students to brainstorm on the best scenario they can imagine for your community—one year, five years, ten years, twenty years, one hundred years, and five hundred years into the future.

# Awareness and Consciousness Expansion

Some people will be part of the problem simply because they are unaware of the consequences. Once they understand the implications of their beliefs and actions, they may think differently.

## 91. Build on Experience

You can develop interest in sustainability through connections with people's everyday experiences.

Be alert to the experiences of your audiences. Start personal and up-close. What item does everyone share in common? Cell phone? Car? Credit card? Put that item in the center of a discussion and ask exhaustive questions as to its resource use and waste streams, pricing and access, social assets, and shadow effects. Is it contributing to a healthier world, greater prosperity for all, and stronger community? Could it be better designed or need it be replaced to meet these goals?

## 92. Take the Ecological Footprint Quiz

Discuss the concept of bio-capacity and whether or not current methods of resource harvesting and waste generation are depleting nature faster than it can regenerate.

Use one person as a case study to analyze an average household's expenditures in the following areas: (1) food, (2) housing, (3) transportation, (4) consumer goods, and (5) services. Next, visit www.myfootprint.org and use your case study for the eco-footprint quiz. Discuss the results, the choices, and options in the five areas. Discuss limits, challenges, and insights of the quiz. As a follow-up assignment, have participants calculate individual eco-footprints for themselves. Adapt this exercise to your subject area.

## 93. Conduct an Ecological Footprint Audit

Use your campus or organization as a laboratory. We can learn much about our surroundings from a sustainability audit.

In *Sustainability on Campus: Stories and Strategies for Change*, Barlett and Chase (2004) offer a number of case studies that describe how infusing sustainability into courses and curriculum can lead to a dialogue about sustainability issues that extends to community, region, and beyond. One experiential learning course entitled "Greening the Campus" led to remarkable responses, often unanticipated, from a diverse set of university leaders, faculty, and students. These responses ultimately set the stage for broader institutional commitment to sustainability issues. Identify those who could conduct a similar audit in your school, college, university, organization, or community.

## 94. Discuss Full-Cost Accounting

Economic growth in the United States is typically reported in terms of Gross Domestic Product (GDP), or the amount spent on goods and services. But it fails to account for the natural resource materials required to produce those goods and services. Use the ecological footprint as a catalyst for discussion about how and why ecological costs should be integrated in the way economic growth is measured and reported.

For example, you can personalize solid waste issues by requiring students to trace the journey of their garbage from its throwaway point to where it is ultimately disposed. This will help them understand and appreciate the energy and potential consequences of their individual decisions as consumers. In her book *Garbage Land: On the Secret Trail of Trash*, Elizabeth Royte traces the environmental, economic, and social costs of waste disposal. Ask students to make a list of all items they introduce into the waste cycle in one day, then a week, and then a month. In addition to the list of disposed items, ask them to estimate the transportation and energy requirements for pick-up, hauling, and dumping. Add a trip to your local waste disposal site, whether it is a landfill or incinerator. Direct observation of volumes of trash can have an immediate impact on how we behave in terms of waste disposal.

# 95. Explore What's in Everyday Products

Calculate the resources needed to make something as simple as a coffee mug. Consider the raw materials as well as the energy required for production, packaging, marketing, and transportation.

Everything has a natural resource origin of plant, animal, or mineral. As countries such as the United States become increasingly urbanized, the connection between people and natural resources becomes shrouded by interstates, cul-de-sacs, and strip malls. We forget about the resources required to support everyday things in our lives. Ask students to select one thing from their daily routine—water bottle, notebook, or article of clothing, for example—and trace it back to its natural resource origins. Consider the raw materials, as well as the energy required to manufacture and transport the final product from the factory to the shelf at the store via truck, boat, plane, and so forth. Think about packaging, marketing, and disposal costs as well.

# 96. Consider Scale and Energy Consumption

Ask students to list all the energy sources they purchase directly (utility bills, fuel for their cars, etc.) for home and transport, and then keep track of their consumption for a month.

Have people find and read their meters (gas and electric) at least once a week. They should convert all fuels to their kWh equivalent for purposes of comparison and then translate these amounts using a 1.1 multiplier for fossil fuels and 3.0 for electricity. For each unit of primary energy they use directly for their car and residence, they can assume that society uses approximately two units more to support them. This "indirect" energy is used for manufacturing, agriculture, offices, infrastructure, and so forth. Individuals can then calculate how much energy would be required for the United States and the world if everyone else used the same amount of energy that they do. Finally, have them compare their own figures to actual U.S. and world energy consumption by finding these numbers at www.eia.doe.gov.

# 97. Identify Services Provided by Nature

Think about the trees along a street's median. Observe wetlands around a subdivision. Feel the topsoil at a local farm. Discuss how a healthy environment provides valuable—yet largely overlooked—benefits.

Nature is sometimes portrayed as being apart from humans, as a place we go to visit for recreational or spiritual reasons. The dependence of more basic needs, such as human health, on the natural environment can be forgotten. Encourage students and other audiences to explore, for example, how trees provide a service to humans through their absorption of pollutants; how wetlands contribute to water quality and flood control; or how predators keep rodent populations in check. Remind everyone that the ecosystems that surround us play an important role in our individual and collective well-being. Web sites for both the Sierra Club (see www.sierraclub.org) and the Nature Conservancy (see www.nature.org) include issues, projects, travel, and feature articles that routinely address the value of nature in supporting human societies. Search the internet for major environmental groups and you will find a rich repository of similar resources.

# 98. Recognize That Size Matters

Identify the various ways that your students or groups could track and question energy use. Katy Janda of Oberlin College draws on the U.S. Census Bureau's 2006 report to make the following points: "A large new house may use energy efficiently and be constructed with healthy materials, but it will often consume more energy and resources than a smaller 'inefficient' home. The general trend in American building has been to consume more energy and resources in the name of making life better. In 1970, two-thirds of new homeowners kept their cool without central air-conditioning; today, central A/C is a standard feature in eighty-three percent of new homes, even in temperate climates. In the last three decades, the size of the average American home has climbed fifty-seven percent—fifteen hundred square feet in 1970; 2,350 square feet in 2004—to say nothing of the proliferation of two- and three-car garages. These examples point to the need for 'sufficiency,' the ability to break the spiral of material saturation that currently signifies affluence and well-being in our society."

Janda uses this exercise to illustrate these concepts: "Students use appliances in a retail store and a handheld diagnostic tool called a Kill-a-Watt to study the relationship between size, efficiency, and consumption in common household appliances like televisions, stereos, and computers. Once permission has been obtained from the retail store manager, students can plug a Kill-a-Watt in series between an appliance and an electrical outlet. An LCD screen displays volts, amps, watts, Hz VA and (if left plugged in) cumulative kilowatt-hours over time. By using the Kill-A-Watt to make invisible flows of energy visible, students are able to compare the real-time consumption of appliances of different sizes and features. Using these data, they can extrapolate the environmental impacts of various product choices and even government policies. This exercise can be used to assess, for instance, whether using an EnergyStar projection television saves more energy than a smaller non-EnergyStar television."

# 99. Look Twice at What's Disturbing

Investigate how what once was determined to be frightening (fire), threatening (predators), or expendable (buffalo) are now understood to have profoundly positive impacts on biodiversity.

For example, because we now understand that fire is an essential player in forest ecosystem health, we are introducing fire-adaptive land management practices. When wolves were reintroduced into Yellowstone National Park, even the willows flourished. New findings on the tall grass prairie show the disturbance that had the greatest impact on biodiversity was grazing by bison as reported by Dan Ferber in Nature Conservancy. Research how these and other missing elements now help us comprehend that natural web of interdependence and sustainability. Share stories that show previously disturbing elements of nature in a new light.

# *Effective Communication*

Complexities and ideals surround sustainability and require deep listening, empathy, and negotiation in order to find common ground, move forward, and avoid violence.

## 100. Widen Participation

Students often complain about the few who tend to dominate classroom discussions. Parallels with public and political arenas are clear: special interest groups and lobbyists dominate discussions about public policy. Develop mechanisms for ensuring wide and sustained participation. Find consensus among your students for new ground rules that encourage equal participation from everyone.

According to author Mary Belenky and her colleagues, "It becomes important for instructors to encourage participation in classroom discussions because it is in this way that students, and females in particular, 'find their voices,' and mature intellectually" (Belenky, Clinchy, Goldberger, and Tarule, 1986, 17). Early in each class, facilitate a discussion of the "ground rules." Get students involved in determining the ways in which they will be expected to participate in class.

# 101. Emphasize Soft Skills and Hard Sciences Equally

Share with students and others the need to balance ideas with the communication of and about those ideas.

Knowledge about ecological processes and biological organisms is imperative to achieving sustainability; knowing how to translate that knowledge for nonscientific individuals and audiences is equally important. For example, a long-term plan to reduce carbon emissions in a community requires knowledge about nutrient cycles and atmospheric sciences; and it also requires that business leaders, citizens, industry representatives, and others cooperate in finding a solution that is workable in the community. Discussions must pair with knowledge in order to make lasting changes. Choose a topic in your community, and talk about how it can be best communicated to and discussed with those who live there.

# 102. Teach How to Negotiate

Dedicate some time in class or with your organization to teach negotiation skills and principles that help people throughout their lives, both professionally and personally, especially when they are pushing for more sustainable solutions to complex problems.

In their classic text on negotiating, *Getting to Yes*, Roger Fisher and William Ury summarize their recommendations in this way: "The method of principled negotiation is to decide issues on their merits rather than through a haggling process…. It suggests that you look for mutual gains whenever possible, and that where your interests conflict, you should insist that the result be based on some fair standards…. [Principled] negotiation is hard on the merits, soft on the people. It employs no tricks or posturing…. [It] is an all-purpose strategy" (Fisher and Ury 1991, xviii–xix). Use *Getting to Yes* or other similar texts to explore negotiation strategies. Then have students role-play all the sides of a conflict in your community, nation, or world.

# 103. Share Like a Friend

Build an authentic connection with your audiences.

David Dimatteo regularly talks to groups about his company's commitment to sustainability: "In my first years of guiding tours at New Belgium Brewing Company, I had never noticed that I was talking at my guests and not with them. One day I started asking what they wanted to see and hear while trying to blend in a few things I had hoped to share. When I started making the tour all about us and not me I realized that we were finally learning together. Don't bore or intimidate your audience with statistics and jargon beyond their reach. Instead, focus on creating a safe, fun, and interactive environment where the teacher becomes a participant. In this setting we can all learn at the level that makes the most sense to us."

# 104. Be Honest

There are so many ways to express your beliefs and desires. When it comes to addressing sustainability, nothing comes across cleaner and more sincerely than honesty.

Share success stories, the places where the challenges were too great, and the paths your organization decided not to go down. This honesty makes for a tangible connection and encourages buy-in. Engage in meaningful conversations and share ideas with those in attendance while recognizing that there really are no "experts." Sustainability is an ongoing process and we are all in it together. Sharing our experiences is part of this process.

# 105. Share What Has Touched You

Look back at your own life and find a time when a book, a class, a workshop, or maybe a statement spoken to you about sustainability really affected you. How did your feelings, beliefs, or ideals change? Rediscover those moments and dive deeper. Reread a book that sparked your interest or hunt down that professor for some follow-up conversations.

Alie Sweany recalls her own journey toward embracing sustainability: "One great example in my life was an Environmental Ethics class I took at Colorado State University back in the late '90s. The class was taught by a now world renowned philosopher of environmental ethics, Holmes Rolston. This class was so life-altering that today, seven years later, I think of the lessons I learned there. The main idea I took is that humans are not separate from other life forms; in fact, we are not superior to an ant, a piece of moss, or a bird. This lesson seems so simple, yet for me it was so profound. This changed my perspective about life, directing many of my lifestyle and career decisions to this day." Look through Rolston's 1988 classic, *Environmental Ethics*, for ideas or questions you could bring into your own class or program.

# 106. Encourage Specificity

Rethink your writing assignments. Ask for more descriptions. Help students and others develop their ability to write in the present, to be more in the moment, to be more engaging.

In his provocative book on writing, *Walking on Water*, Derrick Jensen connects the writer's need to engage the reader with greater focus on descriptors, details, specifics, context, and place: "We as a culture take the same approach to living in Phoenix as in Seattle as in Miami, to the detriment of all of these landscapes. We believe that students can be given standard lesson plans and standard tests, universally applied, to the detriment of all of these students. We turn living wild trees into standardized two-by-fours. We turn living fish into fish sticks. We turn living carrots into carrot sticks. But every carrot is different from every other carrot. Every fish is different from every other fish. Every tree is different from every other tree. Every student is different from every other student. Every place is different from every other place. If we are to remember what it is to be human beings, and if we are ever to hope to begin to live sustainably in place (which is the only way to live sustainably), we will have to remember that specificity is everything" (Jensen 2004, 59–60).

# 107. Encourage All Writing

Urge people to write about sustainability issues for local newspapers. Empower writing groups to use e-mail for sharing draft copies of letters to the editor. Celebrate those who get published. Invite local writers into your classes and meetings to explore related issues.

Healthy, sustainable democratic systems depend upon an informed and active citizenry. Letters to the editors or opinion pieces in local newspapers allow for diverse voices to be heard. Short of getting their own articles or letters published, you can also ask people to write about their experiences, reactions and ideas for embracing sustainability. Sustainability Coordinator Hillary Mizia described her experiences with this: "Prescott College, a college for the liberal arts and the environment in central Arizona, approaches education in an experiential way. Students for all classes, whether dance or mountaineering, are required to keep portfolios. Inside each portfolio is a section for reflections. Students write about how their learning impacts their lives, what connections they see between classes, general thoughts about class content, etc. These reflections become a valuable tool for learning and everyday success." Encourage students to keep sustainability journals.

# 108. Make It Worthy of Media Attention

Get your sustainability news in the news. Whether it is an issue of urgency or a story of success, the general public needs to see it. Raising these issues on the media agenda will ultimately raise them on the public agenda.

For those with a message of sustainability to share, create a public relations campaign. Make contact with media outlets and maintain a positive connection with reporters and others in a position to broadcast your message. Turn your information into materials (such as news releases) the media can use. Make them prewritten and packaged in a way that the media won't have to do much extra work to reproduce them as stories. Make sure that when you are sharing information through a media outlet, such as newspapers, television, and the internet, the information you produce is easy for everyone to understand.

# Cooperation and Collaboration

Conflicts often arise out of concerns for environmental threats and degradation, social injustice and displacement, and economic inequities and unfairness. Finding more sustainable solutions will require that people work together across differences of backgrounds, beliefs, motivations, and values.

## 109. Turn "Bullets" Into "Bridges"

In a competitive culture like that in the U.S., the model for addressing disagreements is the political debate, where tough attacks and determined defenses supposedly help clarify complex issues like sustainability. In truth, these fights can polarize opinions and muddy the waters even further. Shift your debates to bridges of deeper listening as opposing beliefs stretch to understand other viewpoints, common interests, and new solutions.

William Ury's *The Third Side* describes the skills, beliefs, and values that can transform competition into cooperation and avoid unnecessary, destructive conflicts. His travels throughout the world have provided him with some dramatic examples in the very real world: "In the midst of a firefight in the rice paddies between American soldiers and the Viet Cong early in the Vietnam War, six monks walked toward the line of fire. 'They didn't look right, they didn't look left. They walked straight through,' remembers David Busch, one of the American soldiers. 'It was really strange, because nobody shot at 'em. And after they walked over the berm, suddenly all the fight was out of me. It just didn't feel like I wanted to do this anymore, at least not that day. It must have been that way for everybody, because everybody quit. We just stopped fighting'" (Ury 2000, 16–17). What would happen if the developers and the environmentalists put down their "weapons" and found that "radical center" where constructive communication can begin to bridge real differences? Explore issues in your community that could benefit from such an approach.

# 110. Play Games to Illustrate Collaboration

Simulate an activity that emphasizes the importance of working together to achieve a sustainable planet.

Divide students into teams of mock fishery companies that rely on the same ocean for its harvest. Overstate the goal to harvest more fish than any other team during the game. Each team has the option to take up to three units of fish each year. After each team indicates how many units they will harvest in the first year, add the aggregate number of units harvested that year and subtract that from the total units with which the entire group started (begin with five times the number of teams). Play a second round and again compile the total number used. Because fish are a renewable resource, double the number of units remaining at the end of every second year. Most groups will exhaust the resource within five rounds. Play the game a second time, but give one student from each team an opportunity to participate in a brief summit with individuals from other teams. They will usually identify a harvest pattern that keeps the fishery sustainable indefinitely, but with trade-offs. This exercise provides an excellent example for discussion about the value of collaboration, and the economic and social trade-offs of sustainable harvest strategies.

# 111. Create Community Collaborations

Architecture students at the Ecole des Beaux Arts in nineteenth-century Paris completed short, intense problem-solving assignments. The professor wheeled a cart (*charrette*) through the studio classroom to collect the projects, as students frantically worked to complete their solutions. Today's design *charrettes*, or community design workshops, involve interdisciplinary groups—including project stakeholders—collaborating, brainstorming, and setting common goals for proposed projects such as construction of a new school, public library, housing development, or similar effort.

The *charrette* process can work especially well to generate multiple solutions to a local project or issue. For instance, construction, design, and engineering students at Colorado State University worked with junior high students, their parents, and professional architects and engineers in a four-hour *charrette* to envision goals and ideas for a new environmentally friendly charter school. The college students learned from the professionals; the junior high school students offered fresh ideas and gained insights into college and professional careers; and the parents came away with an exciting start to a new school construction project. While assembling such a diverse cast of participants takes organization and coordination, the results illustrate the benefits of synergistic collaboration.

# 112. Design a Better World Together

Each year, as an extra credit experience, a group of college students visits sixth grade classes at an elementary school close to the Colorado State University campus. In a two-hour workshop, the sixth graders are taught about sustainability issues, work in small groups led by college students, and are charged with designing a better world for their future. Using facts obtained from books and online sources, the college students use the first part of the workshop to explain existing and predicted planetary conditions as well as current examples of inventions and activities that illustrate sustainable practices.

In the body of the workshop, each small group is responsible for a topic such as transportation, buildings, food, climate, creatures, or clothing. Each group is asked to (1) list specific issues related to their topic, and (2) brainstorm solutions and related ideas. Large poster paper is used to record the issues; each student is given colored markers and is encouraged to draw their solutions and ideas. The final part of the workshop is reserved to allow the topic groups to present their ideas. Numerous creative, futuristic concepts emerge as elementary and college students collaborate to envision a sustainable future for the planet.

## 113. Tie Classes and Programs Together

Identify what you can do to bind individual classes or programs to some greater message on sustainability. For example, you can focus everyone's attention at the outset on a case study that has implications for environmental, economic, and societal health and how your work can make a difference.

Students often think their classes are taught in a vacuum. One-time workshops or presentations may have only limited value. However, you can help any audience remember key points by showing them how ideas flow together like tributaries of large rivers. Build that picture at the very beginning so everyone understands the importance of his or her efforts and how the information that follows is connected.

## 114. View Conflict as a Change Agent

Rethink the notion that conflict is negative. This reframe is essential to fully engage the many complex and often competing aspects of sustainability.

Author and martial artist Thomas Crum states, "Nature doesn't see conflict as negative. Nature uses conflict as a primary motivator for change. Imagine floating down the Colorado River through the Grand Canyon…truly one of the world's great wonders and [it] provides us with a profound sense of harmony and peace. Yet how was that amazing vista formed? Eons and eons of water flowing, continually wearing away the rock, carrying it to the sea. A conflict that continues to this day. Conflict isn't negative, it just is" (Crum 1987, 31, 49). For example, in Colorado, loggers, mill workers, facilities managers, recycling centers, and renewable energy enthusiasts are now approaching the conflict over forest management—for years a battleground of distrust and litigation—and together crafting community-based projects in bioenergy and green building materials.

# Community and a Sense of Place

While much in our modern lives can remove us from the fabric of community and place, the sustainability movement invites us to become reacquainted with where and with whom we live. Bioregional teaching connects us to the web of natural and human resources we interact with on a daily basis.

## 115. Keep It in the Neighborhood

Read the local newspaper, visit the local planning office, or check web sites of local conservation organizations to identify issues being addressed in your town. Focus on those issues to which students can directly relate.

Many people are aware of diminishing rain forests in the Amazon, but few take action. Yet, if there were a plan to convert a neighborhood park to development, the entire neighborhood would probably intervene. Many people are more engaged with issues that affect their neighborhoods and other places with which they have a direct connection. Restoring the land can help restore ourselves. Begin locally, where you live, work, visit, and play.

## 116. Get Into "We" Mode

De Graaf, Wann, and Taylor define *affluenza* as "a painful, contagious, socially transmitted condition of overload, debt, anxiety and waste resulting from the dogged pursuit of more" (deGraaf, Wann, and Naylor 2001, 2).

Investigate all the ways we can turn the tables on overconsumption. Buy less. Track how conscious spending and "giving twice"—a donation to a favorite charity that gets you a canvas bag you can then gift to someone else—promotes economic sustainability. Seek out handcrafted gifts to support artisans. Buy fair trade items to support community development and enhance biodiversity. Buy secondhand to promote reuse. Shop at locally owned stores to support community services. Support small farmers and help preserve rural livelihoods. Shop with nonprofit organizations to support a variety of educational programs. Develop the habit of asking, "How can I do with less and how can I do even more with less?" List other ways that your campus, community, or organization could "operate in reverse."

## 117. Recognize Waste

Investigate the waste built into our current systems. Examine the Zero Waste standards at www.zwia.org, take the virtual tour at www.zerowaste.org, or discuss the standards of the Global Recycling Council at www.crra.com/grc. Discover if a list of local "resource recovery" efforts are available, including thrift stores, deconstruction storage, recycling, collection stations, and composting. If not, start one.

One colleague trained by the Zero Emissions Research and Initiatives (www.zeri.org) reports: "A typical coffee business uses .02% of the coffee bean to produce a cup of coffee. This means that 99.8% of the coffee bean becomes waste. A so-called green detergent from palm oil uses only five percent of the biomass from the plant; the rest is treated as waste…. Studies show that between a half and three fourths of the materials used in our industrial economy are generated and treated as waste before ever entering the economy." Have students interview local business people to get an idea of how much waste is generated within your community.

# 118. Trace the Roots of Lunch

The following excerpt comes from a study from the University of Essex, England that was reported in *Food Policy*: "The United Kingdom would save $4 billion annually in environmental and traffic costs if all food consumed was locally grown. An additional $2.1 billion would be saved in environmental costs if all food were grown organically. Further, $189 million in environmental costs would be saved if people walked, cycled or used public transit to get to grocery stores and farmer's markets instead of driving" (University of Essex 2005).

Assign participants to list all of the ingredients in their favorite lunch plate, sandwich, or salad. Direct them to find the geographical source of each item and track the distance traveled to their table. Calculate the fuel spent using current prices. Then, identify two local sources—including homemade—of the ingredients. Calculate transportation costs and compare final cost to consumer of these two approaches. Consider the social and environmental cost versus cultural benefit of each approach and discuss the concepts of true-cost accounting and trade-offs.

# 119. Rediscover Local Agriculture

As Bill Vitek writes for *The Land Report*, "[A] civic agriculture, a culture of food production, distribution and consumption that honors local places, respects the health of consumers and rewards small producers for their commitment to quality and stewardship" (Vitek 2005, 5).

Find out if a list exists of local farmer's markets, community supported agriculture (CSAs), food coops, u-pick'ems, restaurants using local foods, and so forth. If not, compile one; if one exists, add to it. You can also search local food policy councils. Create a recipe book that celebrate local, seasonal foods.

# 120. Walk Your Watershed

Set aside social and political boundaries and discover how the vital gift of water shapes our lives.

Use the following resources as inspiration:

- As you orient toward essential, life-sustaining elements, your watershed provides a more accurate address than does your street or avenue. Visit www.epa.gov/surf/ to locate your watershed. Research the location(s) of the headwaters and your river's journey all the way to the ocean. Identify the natural, cultural, historic, economic, and recreational resources of this vast water network.

- Create a map, placing your central activities of work, play, and home in relation to the watershed. Discern how water gets to your faucet and where it goes after you use it for washing, sanitation, and landscape. Interview a range of water professionals to understand current challenges. Many believe that water will be the next oil—that is, a source of major local, regional, and global conflict. Strive to understand the policies and decisions that ensure your—and your grandchildren's—access to clean water.

- Spend time experiencing solitude at a nearby river or lake. Notice plant, bird, and animal life. Note signs of pollution or depletion. Note quality of light, signs of the season. Write a haiku about your time there (first and third lines have five syllables, second line has seven). Knowing the health of our local waters is part of becoming ecologically literate. Making it personal can open us to the reality of dangers to health, habitat, and supply.

# 121. Compost

Some schools and colleges have gotten into connecting the organic waste from their dining halls with teaching, learning, and composting. Out in the community people use grass clippings, raked leaves, and kitchen scraps. Explore options for your campus, business, or organization.

In her research on recycling of clothing, Colorado State University Design and Merchandising graduate student Karyn Madison was fascinated by an article on composting that appeared in the *San Francisco Chronicle*. The article described children in San Francisco who are learning about composting by putting their brown lunch bags, used napkins, and food scraps into compost bins. The program is called "Food to Flowers" and takes organic material from the school lunchrooms to a composting facility that then converts it into fertilizer for farms, landscape firms, and school garden programs. The students, school district, and the city's Department of the Environment divert hundreds of tons of organic material from the local landfill, reducing the daily amount of garbage for the city by several million pounds, and reducing the school district's garbage pick-up costs. Consider how you might incorporate composting into your home, work, or school.

# 122. Think Local, Fun, High-Tech, and Free

Explore the use of Freecycle—an electronic forum to recycle unwanted items—to link local residents who want to swap unwanted goods.

Jill Charboneau, a doctoral student in design and merchandising, found an enjoyable outlet for addressing what was unsustainable in her field at the local level: "Freecycle is similar to eBay without the money. And it is really fun. There is no bidding or payment to be made. It is local. The only catch is that it is fast. After an item is listed, people e-mail the giver if they are interested. The giver decides who will get the item, usually the first responder. Members also list items they need and then wait to see if anyone gets back to them. Membership is free and you must be a member. The website is at www.freecycle.org and joining is quick and easy, only requiring you to dream up a username and password."

# 123. Enlarge Perspectives

Organize a roundtable discussion on the health of your town and local natural areas. Allow people to speak as though they were resident animal and plant species, as well as the soil, water, and air. Allow one person to speak for the local humans.

One educator uses this group work to help participants "shed our human identity and adopt the perspective of others with whom we either share our bioregion or depend upon for sustenance." Discuss if one human can adequately represent the social and economic diversity of the human family or even all humans in your region. Imagine how your city council or your campus administration might be affected by regular representation from your local river, farmland, forest, or ocean.

# Critical and Creative Thinking

Teaching sustainability requires us to abandon historical ways of doing things and to think "outside the box." We must also analyze and synthesize diverse perspectives, adapt to new information and technologies that influence sustainability, and be creative in our problem solving.

## 124. Teach How to Think, Not What to Think

To help people pay attention to what experts tell them, provide the facts about ecological cycles, address the economic and social dimensions of natural resource issues, objectively describe all perspectives, and, finally, allow individuals to draw their own conclusions about what should be done.

In *Beyond Ecophobia*, David Sobel (2005) advises educators to remain objective in teaching about the environment, or we risk losing credibility and becoming *advocates*, not educators. Teach about ecological cycles; the resources necessary to support our daily lives; and the connections between environment, economics, and society. Then, let students draw their own conclusions about the importance of conservation and sustainability. This approach is more compelling and longer lasting than advocating to students about the so-called *right* behavior.

# 125. Get to the Root

Look for opportunities to explore important issues in an active and interactive manner. Probe an issue. Ask questions. Keep digging until you have gotten to the root of something unsustainable.

An aspirin may make the headache go away, but the source of the problem may still persist. Try to discover how some of our "solutions" have addressed only the symptoms, and not the root cause, of a problem. Subsidizing local recycling operations is a solution for community recycling that addresses the symptom of a much larger problem—a lack of consumer demand in a region for goods made from recycled materials. That is an economic and social issue that remains unaddressed by a "solution" of subsidization. And perhaps there is an even deeper issue to be explored…?

# 126. Change Periods Into Question Marks

Learning how to question—to challenge conventional wisdom and rethink the prevailing paradigm—has been a hallmark of learning dating back to the earliest writings of the Greek philosophers. List enshrined beliefs of your own discipline or group and substitute question marks for periods. Note your own reaction as well as how others respond.

In his groundbreaking work on multiple intelligences, Howard Gardner tracks the process by which Charles Darwin struggled with what he had been taught and told in making sense of what he saw on the Galapagos Islands. "Darwin had begun to question the dogma of his time: that species were immutable, created at one fell swoop and essentially unchanging thereafter. Evidence pointed precisely in the opposite direction. Rather than being fixed, there were endless varieties, each seemingly attuned to the niche in which it found itself. Perhaps each had had a common ancestor, which had diversified into different species, each suited to the ecology of a particular island" (Gardner 2000, 163). While there is some debate about the best way to teach critical thinking, everyone agrees that students at every level of schooling should have opportunities to practice higher levels of thought, to analyze, synthesize, evaluate, and apply their learning. You can begin with questions.

# 127. Focus on Imagination

Finding sustainable solutions to tough problems requires a paradigm shift about how we think and act. As teachers, too many of us have a tendency to present facts instead of challenging students to come up with their own ideas. Natural resource management expert Peter Newman often reminds his students of Einstein's words: "Imagination is more important than knowledge." Reevaluate the level of creativity you allow in your classes and presentations.

In *Teaching and Performing*, Timpson and Burgoyne write, "As an instructor, you have a wonderful opportunity—a license, even a mandate—to create and innovate. If your students become bored or listless, are you able to adjust your plans and do something to re-engage them?... In the theatre, actors must recreate and re-energize a production every time the curtain goes up. Creative expression is what brings a script to life. Without that energy and concentration, productions are flat and listless" (Timpson and Burgoyne 2002, 177). Looking through the tips in this book alone will give you a range of energizing and creative options on which to draw. Use your imagination! Stretch your students and groups to consider very different possibilities. Practice thinking outside of your particular box. Focus the energy that results toward new solutions.

# 128. Go for Understanding

Identify cases or problems you can explore as an alternative to content coverage. Utilize some time at the end of a lesson to challenge students to reflect on their learning and share ideas with their classmates. Raise your expectations beyond information acquisition and into understanding and critical thinking.

In *The Disciplined Mind*, Howard Gardner critiques the conventional practices of teachers and schools: "Unwittingly, teachers are complicit in the survival of early, inadequate representations and misconceptions. The villains include a text-test context, in which students are simply examined on the content of texts or lectures, without being challenged to use the information in new ways; short-answer tests, which offer a set of choices, rather than requiring students to create the choices and select among them; and the uneasy but prevalent compromise by which teachers tacitly agree not to push students too hard, as long as students return the favor. And, above all, there is the old devil 'coverage.' So long as one is determined to get through the book no matter what, it is virtually guaranteed that most students will not advance toward genuine understanding of the subject at hand" (Gardner 2000, 122). Find ways to challenge your students—and yourself—to break from a preoccupation with content coverage.

## 129. Study Controversial Issues

The brain is like any other muscle; it needs regular, vigorous exercise. Sustainability demands new and innovative thinking. We can all practice these skills by starting with the data and forming our own conclusions.

Nel Noddings has written much about a culture of care, what is required of individuals and society to create more supportive communities: "If we value critical thinking, if we commit ourselves to encouraging it, then we must allow it to be exercised on critical matters—that is, on issues of keen interest to students.... If we really believe that knowledge and critical thinking contribute to living fuller public and private lives, then we must allow the study and discussion of such critical and controversial issues" (Noddings 2003, 148). When dealing with environmental, economic, and social issues, go beyond the obvious to deeper solutions to complex problems.

## 130. Be a Wide-Eyed Skeptic and Demand Precision

Along the path of sustainability there will be many people trying to sell you different solutions. Some of them may be helpful, some not. Do not willingly accept anything as the *only* answer. Keep your eyes open about all options, and be skeptical when you hear a claim about a simple solution. Reject sloppiness in concepts and demand precision. For example, global warming can never be "cured" by a simple "inoculation" of technology like a hybrid engine.

Because sustainability is a complex, multidisciplinary concept, discussions are more useful when they include references to underlying environmental, economic, and societal factors, definitions, and concepts. For example, in New Orleans, the poorest residents lived in the lowest areas and were the most vulnerable to flooding. It is obvious now that any sustainable solution for that city must address more than the levies. Have students or groups pick an issue in your community and explore the variety of factors involved.

# 131. Investigate Campus Ecology

Many valuable resources are available through libraries, organizations, and web sites. Help students and others develop skills for focusing their investigations, searching through resources, and identifying sustainable solutions.

For example, with its emphasis on promoting sustainability in higher education, Second Nature has developed a treasure chest of materials for teaching, curriculum, institutional policy, and more. See www.secondnature.org. The National Wildlife Federation's work on campus ecology has resulted in a series of Yearbooks that describe what various colleges and universities have accomplished. Explore their web site at www.nwf.org/campusecology. Assign local projects to students that draw on these ideas.

# 132. Blur Lines of Distinction Between Disciplines

Fields of study typically have long histories that are organized, maintained, and ordained by colleges and universities worldwide. Yet real world issues— especially those involving environmental, economic, and social dimensions— are inherently interdisciplinary or transdisciplinary. Look for the interconnections among the fields of studies closest to your own. Create projects that require students to integrate ideas from different subject areas. Embrace the complexities and ambiguities as you look for understanding and sustainable solutions. Universities contain a wealth of knowledge from various disciplines. Call your colleagues in different fields and ask them to speak about their own perspectives on topics that you may be teaching.

For example, in the natural resources management courses at Colorado State University, students often study world heritage sites in Central America that contain cultural resources such as Mayan ruins. They focus on management techniques, interpretation, and protected area planning processes. However, across campus there are professors who study art history of the Maya. By bringing our classes together everyone hears other perspectives and sees the true depth of these issues.

# 133. Use Creative Works to Spark Debate

Creative works of fiction provide engaging ways to debate what is sustainable and what is not. Edward Abbey's *The Monkey Wrench Gang* (1975) and

*A Friend of the Earth* by T. C. Boyle (2000) are two examples of novels rich with useful ideas.

Elementary school teacher and doctoral student Tim Pearson notes that "by using suspense novel A *State of Fear* as a vehicle to convey his skepticism, Michael Crichton conveys his belief that the threat of global warming is overblown. He studied the literature on global warming for two years before beginning this novel and includes an extensive bibliography that chronicles his research. Is he right? Is the data insufficient to point to climatic change caused by human influence? Are nations who have adopted the Kyoto accords acting upon bad science and incomplete data? Are environmental groups using fear to increase their influence and economic standing? Or, is global warming indeed the most significant environmental threat that faces the world today? Crichton's novel could serve as an entertaining and provocative starting point for a discussion of global warming. By beginning with the contrary view, and following the reading with more study, readers are likely to form opinions that are better informed and durable." List novels that could raise important issues in an engaging way and provoke useful discussions within your own field.

# 134. Make Debates Public and Inclusive

Ask students to approach issues of sustainability from a perspective of "public discourse." Challenge them to include perspectives that are often excluded.

A university professor who specializes in school law argues that we should follow certain principles when debating the implications of a move toward greater sustainability: "I like what Baber and Bartlett have to say on this subject in their book, *Deliberative Environmental Politics: Democracy and Ecological Rationality*. First, discourse and debate must be grounded in equality of access and influence, and include those who have not been represented. Second, debate must be based on "good faith" bargaining—that is, people must use public reasons to support their positions. Third, the resolution of sustainability issues should avoid stalemate and obstruction. Discussions of sustainability can be derailed when considered exclusively as matters of private concern. One way we can move beyond the limitations of these perspectives, however, is to adopt the three steps of 'public discourse' outlined above." Have students use these guidelines to discuss a hot-button issue in your community.

# 135. Progress Logically

Assess where people are in their thinking. Mentor them through a progression of development that ultimately leads to changes in thinking and behavior. Be patient, systematic, and rational when encouraging people to understand and draw conclusions about sustainability practices.

In 1977, as the environmental movement gained momentum on our planet, the United Nations convened hundreds of professionals in Tbilisi, Georgia (then USSR) to define goals for educating about the natural world. The final product of that meeting was the Tbilisi Declaration, which defines a sequential process in which educators should (1) make students aware of an issue, (2) provide the facts and knowledge about that issue, (3) help students acquire values and feelings of concern for the environment, (4) provide skills training for identifying and solving environmental problems, and (5) facilitate opportunities to take action. (See National Consortium for Environmental Education and Training's *Defining Environmental Education 1994*.)

# 136. Teach Good Reasoning

Because some people benefit from unsustainable practices, they will often attempt to block changes toward sustainability. This resistance might be attacked with anger, hostility, aggression, and even force. However, it is important to understand that force is, in itself, an unsustainable practice. Wars are inherently destructive and costly. In contrast, good reasoning is sustainable and can be taught.

As an instructor in philosophy, Rod Adams has had much experience with the teaching of critical thinking: "In my Logic and Critical Thinking classes, we learn to distinguish mere assertions from arguments (that is, assertions backed up by reasons); and for the arguments, we learn to objectively distinguish good arguments from bad. This skill of identifying and evaluating arguments is crucial to countering the clever rhetoric of powerful people who, for whatever personal reasons, resist implementing sustainable practices in our design, development, and distribution of material goods. My goal in teaching Logic and Critical Thinking—and I tell this to my students (our emerging voters and decision makers)—is to contribute to elevating the political discourse in this country from personal attacks and ambiguous catch phrases to genuine dialogue about what is best for our nation. Discussions of sustainability fit into that goal."

# Supporting Change

Peter Senge (2000) describes the top schools as reflective communities, able to create a unity of purpose about student learning, skilled in collaboration and open to improvement, engaged in their own ongoing renewal with the guidance of supportive, knowledgeable leadership. Building these qualities into any organization will help cultivate a culture of change. As Easwaran points out, such change can also take place on an individual basis: "Once, when Gandhi's train was pulling slowly out of the station, a reporter ran up to him and asked him breathlessly for a message to take back to his people. Gandhi's reply was a hurried line scrawled on a scrap of paper: 'My life is my message.' It is a message which does not require the vast stage of world politics, but can be put into practice here and now, in the midst of daily life" (Easwaran 1975).

## 137. Lead Reform and (R)Evolution

Change can ripple slowly through a system by sustained effort at reform or explode on the scene with the force of a revolution as new rules, policies, and practices turn things upside down. List the various aspects of sustainability that impact your field. Which have been reform and which revolution? What skills and understanding do your students and groups need for each?

In *Walking on Water*, writing instructor Derrick Jensen struggles with knowing how to think about all the changes he sees as necessary: "I've been stuck on this question of reform versus revolution for years now, and perhaps it's time I finally took my own advice and realized I'm asking the wrong question. Reform versus revolution is a false dichotomy. The first answer is that we need both: Without a revolution, the planet is dead, but if we simply wait for the revolution the planet will still be dead before the revolution comes" (Jensen 2004, 193). Embracing sustainability means embracing change in all its myriad manifestations. Discuss revolutions and reforms that have changed your community.

## 138. Influence Others

Identify one or more issues in your own discipline in which sustainability can be questioned—where environmental, economic, and social factors converge and raise real problems.

Former congresswoman Patricia Schroeder represented Denver in the U.S. House of Representatives for twenty-four years. Over the years she was an effective champion for any number of progressive issues. At the core of her prescriptions for progress on sustainability are informed, engaged citizens. In *Stop the Next War Now*, she states, "In a democracy, an educated electorate is essential. Yes, it takes time, but how else can a democracy flourish? Absolute power does corrupt absolutely in any system. If the people are asleep, uninterested, uncaring, or uninterested, we are in trouble. So the best way to make a difference…is to roll up your sleeves and get to work influencing those around you" (Schroeder 2005, 146–147). List the potential contributions activists could make. Assign students the task of contributing in one of the ways listed.

## 139. Train Activists for Life

Taking a page from activists' activities—from the Civil Rights, peace, and environmental movements—we can help students and others learn to act on their commitment to sustainability. Service learning or volunteer activities, for example, can give people important opportunities to translate their beliefs into action.

In an article for *Yes, A Journal of Positive Futures*, Richard Lang, a pastor of Trinity United Methodist Church in Seattle, notes the important role of training in various progressive movements: "In the 1930s Myles Horton and others created the Highlander Folk School to train people of faith to organize labor in the coal mines and textile factories of the south. In the 1950s, they switched their priority to civil rights, training amongst others Rosa Parks, Martin Luther King, Clarence Jordan (who trained Millard Fuller of Habitat for Humanity), the Freedom Riders, and so on. Highlander, a little jewel in the Appalachian region of Tennessee, was a seed-factory that nurtured and sustained the civil rights movement, and it's still around today working on local issues" (Lang 2006, 31–32). Read about historical and current initiatives at Highlander Center for Research and Education in Tennessee at www.highlandercenter.org. You can also read James Fraser's *A History of Hope: When Americans Have Dared to Dream of a Better Future* for insights into activism in the United States from the very beginning. Study the history of activism in your own field. Discuss what can be done today…and tomorrow.

## 140. Create a Peer Culture of Behavior Change

Develop a forum for students to share their stories and anecdotes with each other about what they are doing to help achieve sustainability. Their enthusiasm can become contagious.

One instructor in natural land use reports, "Each week, I ask students to write down one new behavior from the previous week they did to contribute to sustainability. I read these aloud and, when appropriate, discuss the economic and social advantages of each. I then ask students to select one of the behaviors for a weekly award. In one class, we used a 'green shirt' award that became a coveted prize after it was passed from student to student over the course of many weeks. Each recipient left a mark on the shirt (a patch, a creative accessory) before passing it along to the next person. After a few weeks, students had exhausted the common conservation behaviors (such as shorter showers, recycling newspapers) and had to make an additional effort to earn the green shirt. For example, one student started a recycling program at his workplace; another organized a river clean-up for her residence hall." Try a "green shirt" award in your own class or organization.

# 141. Become the Demand

Make informed choices and you might be surprised at the results.

Sustainability Coordinator Hillary Mizia likes to tell this story: "Did you know that one quarter of all conventional pesticides and chemical fertilizers globally are used on conventional cotton farms? In 1999 we discovered this fact while researching t-shirt suppliers for our brewery. Once realized, this fact was hard to ignore. We looked at the price difference between conventionally grown cotton and organically grown cotton, which uses no pesticides and no chemical fertilizers. At the quantity we were looking to buy, price turned out not to be an issue. The choice was then simple. We switched all label t-shirts to organic cotton. In one fell swoop we had become the nation's largest buyer of blank organic cotton t-shirts. A few years later when we started to do our process flow chart, we realized what a good choice this had been. In 2003 we sold 56,000 label t-shirts." Find similar stories and invite those involved to tell your students or groups. Identify where your choices could drive important changes, and what choices have already done so.

# 142. Envision Change

Use the creative process—metaphorical and imaginary thinking—to imagine Earth before, during, and after human habitation. Pretend that you and your students really are Earth. Imagine how you would feel as toxins are poured into your air and water, as your land masses are routinely scoured for coal and minerals, and overgrazed or oversaturated with chemical fertilizers and pesticides. Use these metaphors to add depth and emotion into discussions and analyses.

High school science teacher Kevin Murray reported that "empathy is a powerful teaching tool. Envisioning the pain of Earth as it experiences these threats to its basic life support systems can help students understand the gravity of the situation and allow them to think about how they can help. Change is more possible with creative solutions. According to Joyce, Weil, and Calhoun, metaphorical thinking introduces conceptual distance and thereby allows new insights to emerge. When we remove our linear minds and our political interests from these complex issues in order to think outside the box, we may be better able to see more sustainable solutions." How are Earth's systems analogous to a human's? What would be the consequences of saturating one's blood stream with a percentage of toxic waste similar to what is dumped into Earth's water systems?

# 143. Use "Team Wonder Bike" as a Model

Encouraging change in behavior is the only way to truly raise awareness and create change. Whether in your school, business, or home, take the time to create change. Find one action, however small, and reward yourself and others for doing it. Research the environmental, economic, and social aspects of this action, and let everyone know the good they are doing for themselves and their community.

New Belgium Brewing Company has long been a conscious environmental steward. Since its inception in 1991, the brewery has followed its heart and done what it feels is the right thing to do for people, profits, and the planet at its facility. As the years passed, New Belgium realized it had the potential to create real change in people's lives *outside* the brewery as well. After examining the various ways New Belgium could help to create change in the world, Team Wonder Bike was released at the Telluride Blue Grass Festival in the summer of 2005. This fun, yet simple, program asks participants to replace one car ride a month with a bike ride for one whole year. Willing parties sign a pledge form and, at the end of the year, one lucky participant wins a limited edition Fat Tire cruiser bike. Based on an honor system, Team Wonder Bike demonstrates to participants the impact they can have on their health, their wallet, and the community by riding instead of driving. By the end of 2005, thousands of people in the United States were members of Team Wonder Bike. What started out as a fun, simple, engaging idea to get people to ride has turned into a successful behavior changing exercise.

# 144. Walk the Talk

Be a model of sustainable behavior. What we model speaks volumes to those watching. We all learn much from observing what others do. Take an inventory of what you, your students, and others—including friends, family, and colleagues—actually do to reduce waste, conserve energy and other resources, and support sustainable solutions—large and small.

Your message about sustainability carries more weight when others observe you practicing what your preach. Have everyone share ideas about being better role models. Demonstrate the importance of sustainable action through your own actions. Role modeling is an important mechanism for leading by example. Even simple gestures get the point across:

- Use double-sided copies for assignments, readings, and exams.
- Recycle waste generated in your office and classroom.
- Use a mug for coffee and use your own tableware for take-out.
- Buy supplies made from recyclable or renewable materials.
- Encourage students to avoid unnecessary and unrecyclable cover pages.
- Turn off lights and computers when you leave a room.
- Take alternative transportation to work, school, and other local destinations.

# 145. Sweat the Small Stuff

Sustainable behavior must become habitual in all parts of our lives—at work, home, and elsewhere. While we have unique opportunities to affect our planet through our teaching, we also have opportunities every day in all aspects of our lives to support sustainability with our decisions and actions.

Figuratively or literally, you can wear your "sustainability hat" in the roles you play, as a teacher, leader, worker, consumer, citizen, neighbor, friend, family member, teammate, and traveler. The cumulative impact of all of us engaging in simple, sustainable actions can be tremendous:

- Consume less and strive for zero waste.
- Shop at locally owned businesses for your goods and services.
- Bring your own bags to the grocery store and buy in bulk.
- Insulate your hot water pipes, seal leaks, and change your furnace filter.
- Buy an alternatively fueled vehicle and keep your tires inflated to the proper level.
- Consolidate errands into single trips.
- Invest in "green funds" or organizations that are sustainability driven (see www.sustainability-index.com/).

# 146. Be a Prayer

In *Ethics for the New Millenium*, the Dalai Lama ends with a prayer that asks us all to participate more actively in what is life affirming (1999):

*May I become at all times, both now and forever*
*A protector for those without protection*
*A guide for those who have lost their way*
*A ship for those with oceans to cross*
*A bridge for those with rivers to cross*
*A sanctuary for those in danger*
*A lamp for those without light*
*A place of refuge for those who lack shelter*
*And a servant to all in need*

# 147. Continue the Tips

The previous 146 tips are not intended to be exhaustive, but more of a starter list of both big and small ideas connected to concrete actions.

There are many more tips to be explored, discovered, created, described, applied, refined, and disseminated. Join us in this important work and teach others what you find useful. Send your ideas and comments to us at *TeachingSustainability@ColoState.EDU.*

# Afterword by Julie Newman

## THE ROLE OF A CAMPUS SUSTAINABILITY PROFESSIONAL IN FACILITATING INSTITUTIONAL REFORM

Campus sustainability professionals are emerging across campuses large and small, public and private, urban and rural, throughout the United States and Canada. We represent a range of educational and professional backgrounds from policy and environmental engineering to natural resource management and law—yet what we have in common is the challenge to reform an institution of higher education framed by the principles of sustainable development. We are hired to facilitate the process of applying sustainability theory to practice within the walls of a university, cutting across curriculum, operations, research, and outreach. To be successful, we must be able to comprehend and overcome organizational barriers as well as engage with and successfully communicate across a diverse community of administrators, faculty, students, and staff. For administrators, this may mean thoughtfully supporting the development and implementation of campus-wide policies that illustrate an institutional commitment to sustainability. For our faculty this

---

*Julie Newman is the Director of the Office of Sustainability at Yale University.*

may mean integrating sustainability discourse across multiple disciplines into their curriculum and, when appropriate, using the campus as a classroom. For our students this may mean developing peer-to-peer education that encourages student behavior in support of sustainable practices. For our staff, this means understanding how an institutional commitment to sustainability manifests in day-to-day decisions.

While our overarching goals may be aligned, our approaches tend to vary from campus to campus for reasons extending from the mundane—such as campus locale, population, and financial support—to the theoretical, such as how sustainability has been interpreted and embraced by the university community and administration. Nonetheless, "best practices" are prevailing and sustainability principles are now being reflected in campus operations across the country. Today we can identify examples of successful transportation demand management systems, on-site renewable energy sources, integrated waste management systems, sustainable procurement practices, local and organic food choices, high efficiency building design and construction standards, and land management practices. Applying sustainability principles to a campus is no longer a question of how a university can afford to do this—but rather a question of innovative solution design, forward thinking, optimization of operational systems, leveraging unit interactions, and valuation of the educational outcomes shaped by these actions.

Those institutions that have accepted the challenge of developing a sustainable campus are coping with numerous critical questions on a daily basis. Examples of these questions include:

- How can the integration of sustainability principles advance the objectives of higher education?
- How would a sustainable educational institution internalize the limitations and capacities of the Earth's natural life support systems?
- How ought the institutional systems and processes be shaped that lead to a sustainable system?
- How do we set about transforming the core values and operational practices of our institutions to incorporate sustainability principles?
- How do we know when our campus is "sustainable"?
- How do we interject this content into courses already stretched with ever growing bodies of information?

- How do I as a Sustainability Director support our faculty in teaching about all these issues across the various disciplines?

These questions illustrate the range of multifaceted issues related to sustainability—including moral and ethical ones—that often require community debate and resolution.

As sustainability educators and practitioners, our responsibility is to foster this dynamic dialogue that leads to the development of applicable short- and long-term solutions. True commitment to sustainable development, however, once realized, has a wide range of benefits that make community investment in its development important and worthwhile. Higher education has not only the opportunity but also the responsibility of preparing today's work force. In 2005, in the United States, sixteen million students were enrolled in both two- and four-year degree programs. This fact alone illustrates the vast impact that an institution of higher education can have nationwide.

As the Director of the Office of Sustainability at Yale University, I have been charged with the task of facilitating the development of a sustainable campus, initially focusing upon operational systems. It is my responsibility to build alliances with administrators, students, staff, and faculty across many disciplines. I must be prepared to effectively communicate on a wide array of issues that span from energy conservation and greenhouse gas reduction strategies to the development of transportation demand management schemes and sustainable building design and construction standards, to integrated waste management systems and education and outreach strategies. Due to this recent commitment, Yale students are now exposed to these critical challenges in their tenure as students. A successful sustainable campus is dependent upon how community members are educated to interact within these operational systems.

Complementing the operational activities, some campuses boast examples of sustainability: majors, curriculum, and interdisciplinary applied research. Internally, every college and university must also wrestle with infusing new content on sustainability into courses and classrooms given the historic role of faculty to determine curriculum and their equally historic protections of academic freedom. With that said, Yale currently has many course offerings that incorporate concepts of sustainability. These courses can be found in the undergraduate program at Yale College and in many of the professional schools, including the School of Management, the School of Public Health, the School of Forestry and Environmental Studies, and the School of Architecture.

Yale's recent commitment to becoming a sustainable university provides an opportunity to engage students from multiple disciplines through formal and nonformal curriculum, research, internships, and volunteer opportunities. Yale's scholarly excellence in fields that contribute to sustainability, combined with its ability to do applied research, places us in a position to advance the national and international dialogue on these critical global issues. As colleges and universities recognize the importance of taking a leadership role in addressing these pressing global issues, together we can advance education and action for sustainable development on university campuses around the world.

# Afterword by Joyce Berry

## UNIVERSITY LEADERSHIP

Sustainability requires leadership at all levels within a university. However, it is specifically a Dean's role to provide the leadership that supports, enhances, and "raises the flag" on sustainability academic programs. A Dean's job is to initiate and carry forward a collaborative vision of the future. For the twenty-first century there is no more urgent vision and mission within colleges and universities than to create and steadfastly work toward a vision of a better, more sustainable, and just world.

Sustainability requires integrating the knowledge base of individual disciplines to create a holistic program that brings together the economic, social, and environmental understanding, practices, and policies of a globally and environmentally connected world. A Dean, by nature of her position, is able to (1) provide the creative forum to bring diverse faculty together to build an integrated program, (2) make available the financial support to departments who then allocate faculty time to teaching new and—most often—team-taught interdisciplinary courses, (3) be a champion of, and give credibility by word and action to, new academic sustainability programs, and (4) align sustainability within the highest priorities of a college or university.

---

*Joyce Berry is Dean of Warner College of Natural Resouces at Colorado State University.*

Universities and colleges significantly differ in their governing structures, funding mechanisms, student bodies, breadth and depth of programs, and constituents. Given the assemblage of these characteristics, sustainability programs will be distinctive and craft richly diverse programs. A land grant university such as Colorado State University has a unique heritage and mission that began in the nineteenth century of serving the combined educational, research, and outreach needs of Colorado citizens. A large land grant university is often neither flexible nor nimble in its ability to quickly initiate new programs or to cross disciplinary boundaries. However, a twenty-first century land grant university is able to bring state-of-the-art environmental research, technologies, and practices not only into the classroom, but also into the global workplace through its professional training, and into corporations by its ability to transfer research into economic development focused on new sustainable business practices.

The most important role of universities and colleges, large and small, is to provide the programmatic leadership that will educate tomorrow's environmental leaders. It is the Dean's responsibility to provide leadership that will establish and legitimize academic sustainability programs within a college or university, and to create a cadre of partners and constituents who will bring additional intellectual, experiential, problem-solving, and resource support. Only by establishing teaching sustainability as a broad-based, and outward-focused leadership endeavor will we be able to attain our ultimate goal of a better, more sustainable, and just world.

# *Afterword by Hillary Mizia*

## SUSTAINABILITY GODDESS

Creating change in the business world is not an easy task. It's like an interpretive dance, where one person hears the music of sustainability, feels the beat, and then moves to that beat the best way she or he sees fit. With each business creating its own moves, the dance floor can look like a beautiful creative flow of movement, or like a chaotic series of flailing parts. In an effort to create a few solid dance steps, certain tools and concepts for getting businesses to think sustainably have been developed over the years. The Natural Step, LEED and all its glorious categories, natural capitalism, corporate social responsibility reports, and third party verifiers for those reports are just a few. Each one of these tools, or dances, has been extremely helpful in raising awareness within the business community about what it means to think sustainably and how to move gracefully forward with sustainability in mind. However, none of them can be successful in a business without a champion—a steward who will see them through the initial phases. Without this person, none of these wonderful dance steps will stick, and the dance floor will remain chaotic and cluttered.

---

*Hillary Mizia is the Sustainability Coordinator at the New Belgium Brewing Company.*

One of the most powerful moves a business can make to keep its eye on sustainability is to have a full-time position dedicated to making it happen. Consultants can, and most likely will, also be hired. Yet without the full-time persistence of someone on staff, any sustainability initiative will lose momentum. Something as personal and internally focused as sustainability needs a home within a business. Without that home it is hard for employees to understand and feel the importance of sustainability and all its gifts. At a place like New Belgium Brewing Company we have a lot of stories to share. We have a lot of research to do in order to stay sustainability minded. There are customers, friends, vendors, and other businesses, as well as employees, with a lot of questions about what we do. It has become important to have a person who can address these challenges head-on while staying well-connected to the community in which the brewery functions.

I am currently that person at New Belgium. I was not hired into this position, however. Having been with the company for almost six years, I have been the Sustainability Coordinator for over four. When I began at New Belgium in 2000, there was no such position. I started in what is now known as the Liquid Center—the tasting room that serves as a hub for visitors seeking both high quality beer and information. Working in that department allowed me to feel the pulse of what interested our visitors, and increasingly people wanted to know about our sustainability efforts.

We saw a high number of requests for information and presentations on New Belgium's use of wind power and the like. A year and a half into my job in the Liquid Center, I proposed a Sustainability Outreach Coordinator position. This position would answer questions, give presentations, conduct tours, and maintain a few documents about New Belgium's sustainability efforts, all with the sense of humor and authenticity that makes New Belgium the uniquely community minded company it is. Over the years, this position has moved departments (from Marketing to Employee Health and Safety), changed titles (dropped the "Outreach") and shifted focus, as required. What started out as primarily a way to show people our interpretive dance of sustainability has morphed into reexamining that dance and starting to write down the steps so it may continue for many years as a dynamic force within the company.

As various groups of people look at our brewery, both from the inside and the outside, they see the value we place on sustainability just as they see the value we place on the quality of our beer. The impact of having a person dedicated to the well-being of sustainability in all of its ways is impressive. It says that we are serious about what we do and how we act as citizens of the planet. It also says that we recognize the need to stay on our toes, to keep moving forward with the dance of sustainability as we see fit.

When it was created, this new position called out for a title that would pique curiosity and create awareness; one that expressed the importance with which the brewery embraces sustainability, and that also reflected the lack of seriousness with which we take ourselves. Sustainability Goddess suggests the awe with which we view all that can be accomplished through sustainability, as well as the playful way it can be supported within our company. The job has become part of the fabric of the company. Just as we value the quality of beer, and thus have a quality department, we value sustainability and have a Sustainability Goddess.

# *Final Reflections*

Writing this book has been challenging, difficult, exasperating, and fun. Coming from diverse fields and backgrounds, the glue has been our collective commitment to the idea of sustainability, and our understanding that our present policies, practices, and lifestyles are unsustainable. We consciously chose to pursue synergy as an energizing force that would propel us beyond our individual expertise and into that larger potential that groups possess.

*Bill Timpson* comes from a professional life in education and research to present ways we can teach the skills needed to address today's compelling problems. At the conclusion of this collaboration, Bill noted, "I am indebted to my colleagues and my students for joining me in this bold adventure. The issue of sustainability is so big and complex that the very idea of a concise book of practical tips for teaching it seems, at first glance, impossible, naïve, overly simplistic. Yet we all came to believe that—done well—this book could be a valuable contribution to anyone concerned about waste and pollution; energy conservation; consumption; truths about Earth's finite resources and carrying capacity; and the reality of population growth and ever increasing demands for production."

*Brian Dunbar* is an educator and practitioner focused on green building. For him, this book was "at times refreshing, difficult, surprising, daunting, and provocative. A collection of contributors from disparate fields has worked organically to mold this brief compendium of teaching methods and exercises.

It has been interesting and satisfying to see so many disciplines engaged in developing these strategies. We hope educators can use it to teach learners about the biggest challenge humanity faces: sustaining the planet and all its creatures for future generations."

*Gailmarie Kimmel* brings thirty years as a community educator and has built bridges between various groups—environmental, academic, non-profit, and commercial—to achieve more sustainable solutions. She adds, "For me, underneath concepts and strategies, sustainability is a matter of the heart and how willing we are to be on intimate terms with life. How ready we are to honor the air we breathe, the soil that brings us food, and our bodies that require both. How open we are to interconnect with the poor and homeless, the vanishing and endangered, the weeds, pests, and polluters. Feeling genuinely interconnected with this vastly elegant mystery called Life—and creatively engaging it despite our overwhelm—are at the core of teaching and learning sustainability, and of an empowered spirituality."

*Brett Bruyere* directs the Environmental Learning Center in Fort Collins, CO and teaches courses in natural resource management. For him, this book is an extension of his work: "I genuinely worry about where this planet is headed. Everything in our lives—everything—has its origins in plant, animal, or mineral sources. And our planet simply doesn't have the plant, animal, and mineral resources to sustain the current trends of more and more people consuming more and more resources. Something will have to change. That something, I believe, is the human will to live within our means; that is, to live sustainably. Participating in the compilation of this book provided a compelling reminder that we have educators teaching and affecting thousands of lives every day. They reside in all sectors of our community—private, public, and non-profit—and they come from all kinds of disciplines. Together, with this varied group of educators, we are nurturing the creation of a collective will to live within the resources that the planet provides."

*Peter Newman* teaches and studies the intersection of ecology with human culture, researching protected land management in the Americas. He notes, "Our educational systems have traditionally pushed us to see the world as disciplinary. College campuses are typically organized by discipline and we often find some environmental science-related faculties separated by buildings and hallways. Unfortunately, too many want to treat questions through that narrow disciplinary lens. Yet, we now recognize that environmental issues are not just about the environment. The complexities involve all aspects of life and all disciplines. The broader concept of sustainability challenges us to see the complexities that make life so rich. This book was both a complex and rich experience that brought together people from all across campus into a common space in order to find a common language for integrating aspects of sustainability into our teaching. Each of us now has the responsibility to get these ideas back out across all those various disciplinary aspects of the academy."

*Hillary Mizia* is the Sustainability Coordinator for New Belgium Brewing Company. For her, this book was an exciting partnership. As the work on this book came to an end, she came to the following insights: "When I was approached about this book the wheels began to turn. 'This is something I can write about,' I thought. In reality, my time with this book has meant much more than writing. It has been a time to work with others to create a text full of synergy and hope. It has rekindled passions that were sparked during my undergraduate days, started to burn brighter during my graduate studies, and were glowing upon completion of my thesis and formation of my job at New Belgium Brewing Company. Working with some of my already favorite people, and meeting new favorite people, beginning this dialogue has been a dream come true."

# *Appendix*

The authors pose in front of New Belgium Brewing Company in Fort Collins, CO. From left to right, Peter Newman, Brett Bruyere, Gailmarie Kimmel *(front)*, Bill Timpson *(back)*, Hillary Mizia with baby Miles, and Brian Dunbar.

Group walks through nature centers (such as the CSU Environmental Learning Center in Fort Collins, CO, pictured here) and preserves physically connect students and the environment.

The lobby of LEED certified Fossil Ridge High School in Fort Collins, CO. Students enjoy and perform better in daylit, sustainable schools.

CSU travel courses on sustainability topics, like this one to Maho Bay, St. John, Virgin Islands National Park, help students internalize the importance of focusing on current and future planetary issues.

# References

Abbey, Edward. 1975. *The monkey wrench gang*. Philadelphia: Lippincott.

———. 1991. *Every river I touch turns to heartbreak*. In *Learning to listen to the land*. Washington D.C.: Island Press.

Abelson, Tear, and Great Cowan. 2003. *Parenting partnerships*. In *Making peace*. Bainbridge, WA: Yes.

Alter, Jonathon. 2005. *The other America*. Newsweek 1942–48.

Ausubel, David. 1963. *The psychology of meaningful verbal learning*. New York: Guine and Stratton.

Baber, Walter, and Robert Bartlett. 2005. *Deliberative environmental politics*. Cambridge, MA: MIT Press.

Barlett, Peggy, and Geoffrey Chase. 2004. *Sustainability on campus*. Cambridge, MA: MIT Press.

Belenky, Mary, Blythe Clinchy, Nancy Goldberger, and Jill Tarule. 1986. *Women's ways of knowing*. New York: Basic Books.

Benyus, Janine. 1997. *Biomimicry*. New York: HarperCollins.

Bloom, Benjamin, M. Engelhart, E. Frost, W. Hill, and D. Krathwohl. 1956. *Taxonomy of educational objectives, handbook I*. New York: Longman Green.

Bohman, James. 1996. *Public deliberation*. Cambridge, MA: MIT Press.

Bopp, Michael, and Julie Bopp. 2002. *Recreating the world*. Cochrane, Alberta: Four Worlds Press.

Boulding, Elise. 2005. *Choosing peace*. In *Stop the next war now*. San Francisco: Inner Ocean, 41.

Boyle, T. C. 2000. *A friend of the earth*. New York: Penguin Putnam.

Brown, Lester. 2003. *Plan B*. New York: Norton.

Bullard, Robert. 2005. *Race and poverty are out of the closet*. Sierra (November/ December): 28–29.

Chomsky, Noam. 2005. *Imperial ambitions*. New York: Metropolitan.

Clark, Christopher. 1995. *Thoughtful teaching*. London: Teachers College Press.

Crum, Thomas. 1987. *The magic of conflict*. New York: Simon and Schuster.

David Suzuki Foundation. 2004. *Sustainability within a generation.* Available from web site address www.davidsuzuki.org/files/WOL/Sustainability.

deGraaf, John, David Wann, and Thomas Naylor. 2001. *Affluenza.* San Francisco: Berret-Koehler.

Dewey, John. 1963. *Experience and education.* New York: Collier.

Diamond, Jared. 2005. *Collapse.* New York: Viking.

Earth Charter Initiative. 2000. *The Earth charter.* Available from web site address www.earthcharter.org/files/charter/charter.pdf.

Eitington, Julius. 1996. *The winning trainer.* 3d ed. Houston, TX: Gulf Publishing.

Emoto, Masaru. 2004. *The hidden messages in water.* Hillsboro, OR: Beyond Words Publishing.

Easwaran, Eknath. 1975. *Gandhi the man.* Petaluma, CA: Nilgiri Press.

Ewen, Stuart. 1986. *All-consuming images.* New York: Basic Books.

Ferber, Dan. 2005. *Nature Conservancy* (Winter).

Fisher, Roger, and William Ury. 1991. *Getting to yes.* New York: Penguin.

Flick, Deborah. 1998. *From debate to dialogue.* Boulder, CO: Orchid.

Ford, Peter. 2005. *Egalitarian Finland most competitive, too.* Christian Science Monitor (October 26): 1–7.

Fournier, Ron. 2005. *Politicians failed storm victims.* Newsview (retrieved September 1).

Fraser, James. 2002. *A history of hope.* New York: Palgrave.

Freire, Paulo. 1975. *Pedagogy of the oppressed.* New York: Continuum.

Freire, Paulo. 1983. *Pedagogy in process.* New York: Continuum.

Fullan, M. 2001. *Leading in a culture of change.* Thousand Oaks, CA: Corwin.

Gardner, Howard. 2000. *The disciplined mind.* New York: Simon and Schuster.

Gilligan, Carol. 1982. *In a different voice.* Cambridge, MA: Harvard University Press.

Gladwell, Malcom. 2002. *The tipping point.* Boston: Back Bay Books.

Goleman, Dan. 1994. *Emotional intelligence.* New York: Bantam.

Gorbachev, Mikhail. 2005. *Foreword to State of the world 2005.* Washington, D.C.: Worldwatch Institute.

Gutmann, Amy, and Dennis Thompson. 2004. *Why deliberative democracy?* Princeton, NJ: Princeton University Press.

Hanh, Thich Nhat. 1988. *The sun my heart.* Berkeley, CA: Parallax Press.

Hawken, Paul. 1993. *The ecology of commerce.* New York: HarperCollins.

Hawken, Paul, Amory Lovins, and L. Hunter Lovins. 1999. *Natural capitalism.* Boston: Little Brown.

Huckle, John. 1996. *Realizing sustainability in changing times.* In *Education for sustainability.* London: Earthscan.

Jensen, Derrick. 2004. *Walking on water.* White River Jct., VT: Chelsea Green Publishing.

Joyce, Bruce, Marsha Weil, and Emily Calhoun. 2004. *Models of teaching.* Boston, MA: Allyn and Bacon.

Keyssar, Alexander. 2005. *Reminders of poverty, soon forgotten.* The Chronicle of Higher Education (November 4): B6–B8.

King Jr., Martin Luther. 1963. *Letter to fellow clergy, 16 April.* Available from web site www.almaz.com.

Knapp, Clifford. 1999. *In accord with nature.* Charleston, WV: Clearinghouse on Rural Education and Small Schools.

Kneller, Jane. 2003. *Recalling the canon.* In *Teaching diversity.* Madison, WI: Atwood Publishing.

Kohlberg, Lawrence. 1981. *The philosophy of moral development.* New York: Harper and Row.

Korten, David. 2002. *Living economies for a living planet.* Available from web site www.pcdf.org/living_economies/.

LaDuke, Winnona. 2002. *The Winona LaDuke reader.* Stillwater, MN: Voyageur.

Lama, Dalai. 1999. *Ethics for a new millennium.* New York: Riverhead/Penguin.

Lang, Richard. 2006. *The prophets versus empire. Yes: A Journal of Positive Futures (Winter)*: 29–32.

Leopold, Aldo. 1949. *A Sand County almanac.* New York: Oxford University Press.

Lerner, Steve. 1997. *Eco-pioneers.* Cambridge, MA: MIT Press.

Lloyd, Marion. 2005. *Gardens of hope on the rooftops of Rio.* Chronicle of Higher Education (October 14): A56.

Lomborg, Bjorn, ed. 2004. *Global crises, global solutions.* London: Cambridge University Press.

Louv, Richard. 2005. *Last child in the woods.* Chapel Hill, NC: Algonquin Books.

Lyons, Oren. 1996. *Ethics and spiritual values and the promotion of environmentally sustainable development.* Akwesasne Notes New Series (Winter 1996): 88–93.

Mandela, N. 1994. *Long walk to freedom.* Boston: Little Brown.

Martin, Kelly. 2005. *Evacuees, officials want probe into slow response to hurricane.* HoustonChronicle.com (September 10). Available from web site www.chron.com.

McDonough, William, and Michael Braungart. 2002. *Cradle to cradle.* New York: North Point Press.

McKenzie-Mohr, Doug, and William Smith. 1999. *Fostering sustainable behavior.* Gabriola Island, BC: New Society Publishers.

McKibben, William. 2003. *Enough.* New York: Henry Holt.

McConnell, Carolyn, and Sarah Ruth van Gelden. 2003. *Making peace.* Bainbridge, WA: Yes.

Meadows, Donella. 1997. *Places to intervene in a system.* Whole Earth Review (Winter).

National Consortium for Environmental Education and Training. 1994. *Defining environmental education.* Dubuque, IA: Kendall Hunt.

National Council of Churches USA. 2000. *Ecumenical witness for peace, justice & sustainability.* Available from web site www.ncccusa.org/about/millpeace.html.

National Research Council. 2000. *Inquiry and the national science education standards.* Washington D.C.: National Academy Press.

Noddings, Nel. 2003. *Happiness and education.* New York: Cambridge University Press.

Noon, Paige. 2005. *Material pursuits seem to replace humanity.* Coloradoan, 21 September.

Orr, David. 1992. *Ecological literacy.* Albany, NY: State University of New York Press.

———. 1994. *Earth in mind.* Washington, D.C.: Island Press.

———. 2004. *The last refuge.* Washington, D.C.: Island Press.

Perry, W. 1999. *Forms of intellectual and ethical development in the college years.* San Francisco: Jossey-Bass.

Raffensperger, Carolyn. 2005. *The precautionary principle.* Bioneers Letter (Fall/Winter): 4.

Renner, Michael. 2005. Security. *In State of the world.* New York: Norton.

Robèrt, Karl-Henrik. 2002. *The natural step.* Gabriola Island, BC: New Society Publishers.

Rolston, Holmes. 1988. *Environmental ethics.* Philadelphia: Temple University Press.

Royce, D. 2001. *Teaching tips for college and university instructors.* Needham Heights, MA: Allyn & Bacon.

Royte, Elizabeth. 2005. *Garbage land.* New York: Little Brown and Company.

Ryan, John, and Alan Durning. 1997. *Stuff.* Seattle, WA: Northwest Environment Watch.

Salazar, Alper. 2001. *Sustaining the forests of the pacific coasts.* Vancouver, BC: University of British Columbia Press.

Schroeder, Patricia. 2005. *On not passing the buck. In Stop the next war now.* San Francisco: Inner Ocean.

Senge, Peter. 2000. *Schools that learn.* New York: Doubleday.

Sobel, David. 2005. *Beyond ecophobia.* Great Barrington, MA: Orion Society.

Spotts, Peter. 2005. *Satellite images reveal Amazon forest shrinking faster.* The Christian Science Monitor (October 21): 4.

Takaki, R. 1993. *A different mirror.* Boston: Little Brown.

Tannen, Deborah. 1994. *Gender and discourse.* New York: Oxford.

———. 1998. *The argument culture.* New York: Random House.

Thompson, Richard, and Stephen Madigan. 2005. *Memory.* Washington, D.C.: Joseph Henry Press.

Timpson, William. 1999. *Metateaching and the instructional map.* Madison, WI: Atwood Publishing.

———. 2001. *Stepping up.* Madison, WI: Atwood Publishing and Cincinnati, OH: Thomson Learning.

———. 2002. *Teaching and learning peace.* Madison, WI: Atwood Publishing.

Timpson, William and Paul Bendel-Simso. 1996. *Concepts and choices for teaching.* Madison, WI: Atwood Publishing.

Timpson, William and Suzanne Burgoyne. 2002. *Teaching and performing.* 2d ed. Madison, WI: Atwood.

Timpson, William, Ray Yang, Evelinn Borrayo, and Silvia Sara Canetto. 2005. *147 tips for teaching diversity.* Madison, WI: Atwood Publishing.

Timpson, William, Silvia Canetto, Ray Yang, and Evelinn Borrayo, eds. 2003. *Teaching diversity.* Madison, WI: Atwood Publishing.

Tutu, Desmond. 1999. *No future without forgiveness.* New York: Doubleday.

Ulrich, Thomas. 2005. *How computer maps will help the poor.* The Christian Science Monitor (October 12): 13–15.

University of Essex. 2005. *Food policy* (March).

Ury, William. 2000. *The third side.* New York: Penguin.

Vitek, Bill. 2005. *The Land Report* (Summer): 82. Salina, KS: The Land Institute.

Wackernagel, Mathis, and William Rees. 1996. *Our ecological footprint.* Gabriola Island, BC: New Society Press.

Wheatley, Margaret. 2001. *Leadership and the new science* (revised). San Francisco: Barret-Koehler.

Worldwatch Institute. 2005. *State of the world 2005.* New York: Norton.

# Tip Index

*Note: Numbers below indicate in which tip the topic can be found.*

Adaptation 10, 12, 71, 76, 92, 99

ADD 10

Affluenza 116

Baby Steps 28,144

Biomimicry Section 5, 19, 20, 32, 33, 40, 77, 106

Building 1, 20, 22, 23, 25, Sections 4-5, 41, 46, 64, 70, 82, 89, 98, 112, 133

Change 3, 12, 15, 17, 26, 52, 56, 87, 93, Section 17

Challenge Beliefs 73, 88, 109

Classic Environmentalists 7, 42

Classroom Climate 59, 84, 88, 140, Section 11

Code of Ethics 49, 105, 147

Collective Responsibility 9, 46

Compost 117, 121

Commitment 58, 103, 119, 139

Communication 3, 47, 48, 53, 56, 65, 83, 86, 109, Section 13, Section 16

Complexity 15, 69, 76, 130, 131

Concept Mapping 15

Conflict Resolution 88, 101

Consumption 22, Section 4, 93, 96

Critical Thinking 77, 86, 91, 118, 128, 129, 136, Section 16

Democracy 5, 16, 28, 42, 45, 60, 131, 132, 134, 138

Ecological Footprint 22, 92, 93, 94

Eco-tourism 82

Education 27, 35, 39, 45, 46, 54, 61, 63, 64, 65, 66, 68, 69, 83, 84, 89, 91, 96, 107, 116, Section 16

Efficiency 10, 20, 24, 35, 46, 98

Empathy 45, 86, 142

Evolution 6, 10, 48, 62, 131, Section 17

Future Generations 18, 41, 47

Freecycle 122

Games 12, 70, 74, 76, 78, 79, Section 9, 110

Globalization 11

Green Revolution 11, 23, 25, 31, 38, 41, 70, 93, 98, 117, 133, 140, 145

Happiness 44, 88

Hope 6, 19, 46, 56, 65, 90, 91, 106

Indigenous Peoples 5, 8, Section 2, 41, 48, 50

Inspiration 21, 50, 55, 71, 142

Intuition 72

Knowledge 4, 7, 11, 15, 64, 91, 101, 123, 127, 129

Landfills 13, 16, 94, 121

Leadership 57, Section 17, 71, 86, 101, 136

Local Community 107, 111, Section 15

Marketing 15, 31, 37

Moral Reasoning 124, 125, 134, 136

Natural Disasters 9, 13, 17, 67, 90

Needs vs. Wants 2, 8, Section 4, 30, 44, 57, 60, 73, 75, 97, 124

Networking 34, 123, 132, 138, 146

New Belgium Brewing Company 3, 15, 37, 55, 103, 143

Optimism 102, 110, 147

Peace 6, 8, 19, 43, 45, 50, 88, 114, 139

Perseverance 59, 147

Planning 19, 20, 60, 59, Section 8, 115

Polarization 45, 69, 100, 109, 129, 133, 134

Questioning 8, 16, 41, 44, 61, 63, 64, 66, 68, 79, 98, 105, 125, 126, 137, 138

Recycled Goods 26, 37, 82, 117, 122, 125, 140, 144

Reframing 1, 19, 27, 32, 33, 36, 45, 65, 79, 114

Seventh Generation 41

Social Justice 9, 13, 16, 29, 45, 50, 52, 139

Stewardship 39, 119

Superiority Over 8, 100, 103, 105

Teamwork 80, 112

Technology 4, 24, 35, 54, 62, 63, 73, 90

Terrorism 8, 45

Triple Bottom Line 1, 55, 75

Tutu, Desmond 45

Urban Sprawl 20, 84

Voice 7, 18, 32, 63, 100, 107

Waste 12, 15, 17, 20, 22, 25, 55, 59, 60, 78, 92-94 98, 116, 117, 121, 144, 145

Water 2, 15, 16, 20, 25, 29, 30, 32, 36, 38, 41, 46, 55, 67, 93, 94, 97, 109, 114, 120, 123, 142, 145

Wealth 20, 32, 53, 117

Web of Life 2, 43, 74, 76, 81, 118

Wisdom 5, 47, 48, 126

Women 7, 11, 52